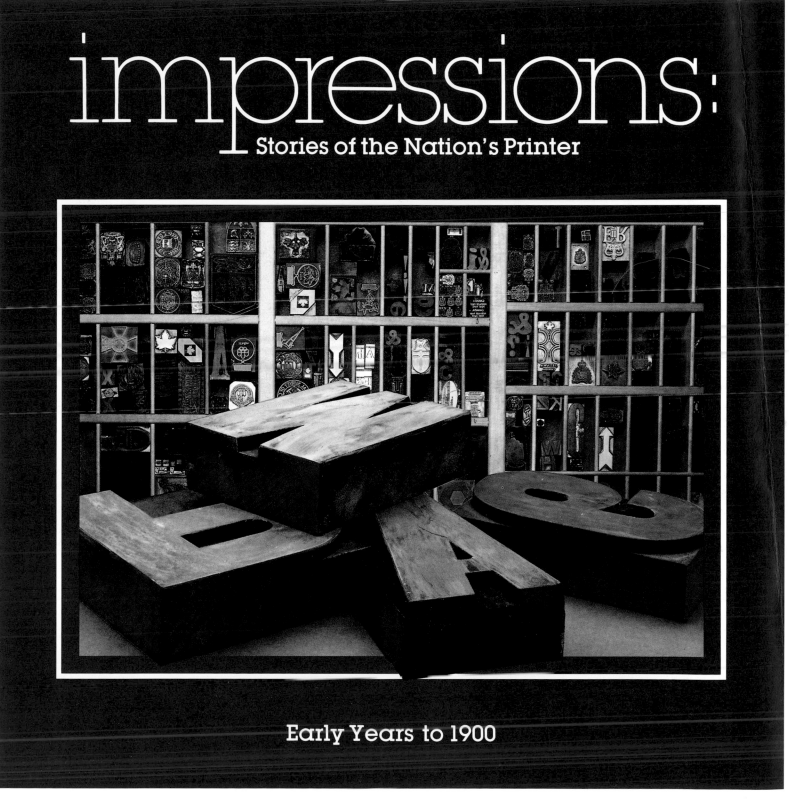

impressions:
Stories of the Nation's Printer

Early Years to 1900

Minister
Supply and Services Canada
Ministre
Approvisionnements et Services Canada

Canada

Produced for the occasion
of the Centennial of the Queen's Printer
for Canada.

Published by the
Canadian Government Publishing Centre,
Supply and Services Canada.

Research and Writing	Hana K. Aach
Project Management	James Riordan, Carol Rutherford
Project Officer	Doreen Ward Keogh
Technical Advice	Clive Benedict
Editorial Assistance	Bianca-F. Bertrand (French)
Production	Terry Denovan
Design	Acart Graphic Services Inc.
Adaptation	Les Entreprises Hélène Bruyère Enr.
Typesetting, Printing, Binding	Canadian Government Printing Services

Canadian Cataloguing in Publication Data

Aach, Hana, 1952-

Impressions: stories of the Nation's Printer, early years to 1900

Issued also in French under title
Impressions: la petite histoire de l'imprimeur national, de l'époque des pionniers à l'année 1900

Includes bibliographical references.
ISBN 0-660-12110-7
DSS cat. no. P35-30/1-1990 E

1. Printing, Public — Canada — History.
2. Canada — Government publications. I. Canadian
Government Publishing Centre. II. Title.
III. Title: Stories of the Nation's Printer, early years to 1900.

JL186.A2214 1989   070.5'95'0971   C90-097093-9

PRINTED AND BOUND IN CANADA

ISBN 0-660-12110-7
DSS cat. no. P35-30/1-1990 E

ACKNOWLEDGEMENTS

Many people and organizations contributed to the process of making *Impressions* a reality. Thanks to the staff of the following institutions, who provided information and often went out of their way to be helpful: the National Library of Canada; the National Archives of Canada; the National Museum of Science and Technology; the Thomas Fisher Rare Book Library at the University of Toronto; the Notman Photographic Archives of the McCord Museum of Canadian History; the Ottawa Public Library and the Bytown Museum. Thanks also to Harold Sterne for permitting the reproduction of illustrations from the publications.

Special thanks to former Queen's Printer Edward (Ed.) Roberts, whose understanding of this organization's history and of the printing industry made his advice and suggestions on the manuscript invaluable.

Grateful acknowledgement to former employees of the Printing Bureau, and to descendants of Queen's Printers and other departmental officials, for giving freely of their time to provide helpful information and for lending precious family papers and photographs. Particular appreciation to Gordon Victor Armstrong, Janet Desbarats, Peter Desbarats, Pierre Desjardins, Peter Larochelle, Frances Hughes, Stewart Hughes and Wilson Macdonald.

Finally, *Impressions* could never have been written without the generous support of the staff of the Communications Services Directorate who, in many different ways, shared their knowledge and expertise acquired during years of service.

A MESSAGE FROM THE QUEEN'S PRINTER

On June 2, 1886, an Act of Parliament first placed Canada's Queen's Printer at the head of a new government department. To commemorate this occasion, we commissioned a project to gather information on the history of our organization. *Impressions* is our way of sharing the results with employees of the Printing Bureau, their families and friends, and with our clients and business associates.

This volume highlights a number of milestones in the development of government printing and chronicles events and circumstances which led to the creation of the Office of Queen's Printer shortly after Confederation and later, to the establishment of the Department of Public Printing and Stationery.

Many of the important challenges and opportunities the Printing Bureau faced during its early years bring to mind striking similarities to our situation today. Then as now, the "Bureau's" success was built on the ability to adapt new technology, and develop new approaches, to enhance its service. This flexibility, to meet the changing needs of the Parliament and Government of Canada, while respecting the abilities of the printing and graphic arts industries, has permitted the evolution of our organization.

We have achieved another milestone — the 100th anniversary of the opening of Canada's Printing Bureau, in October, 1889 — and we can each take a measure of pride in the accomplishments of our predecessors. It is to those talented men and women who helped shape our colourful past, that *Impressions* is dedicated.

Norman Manchevsky

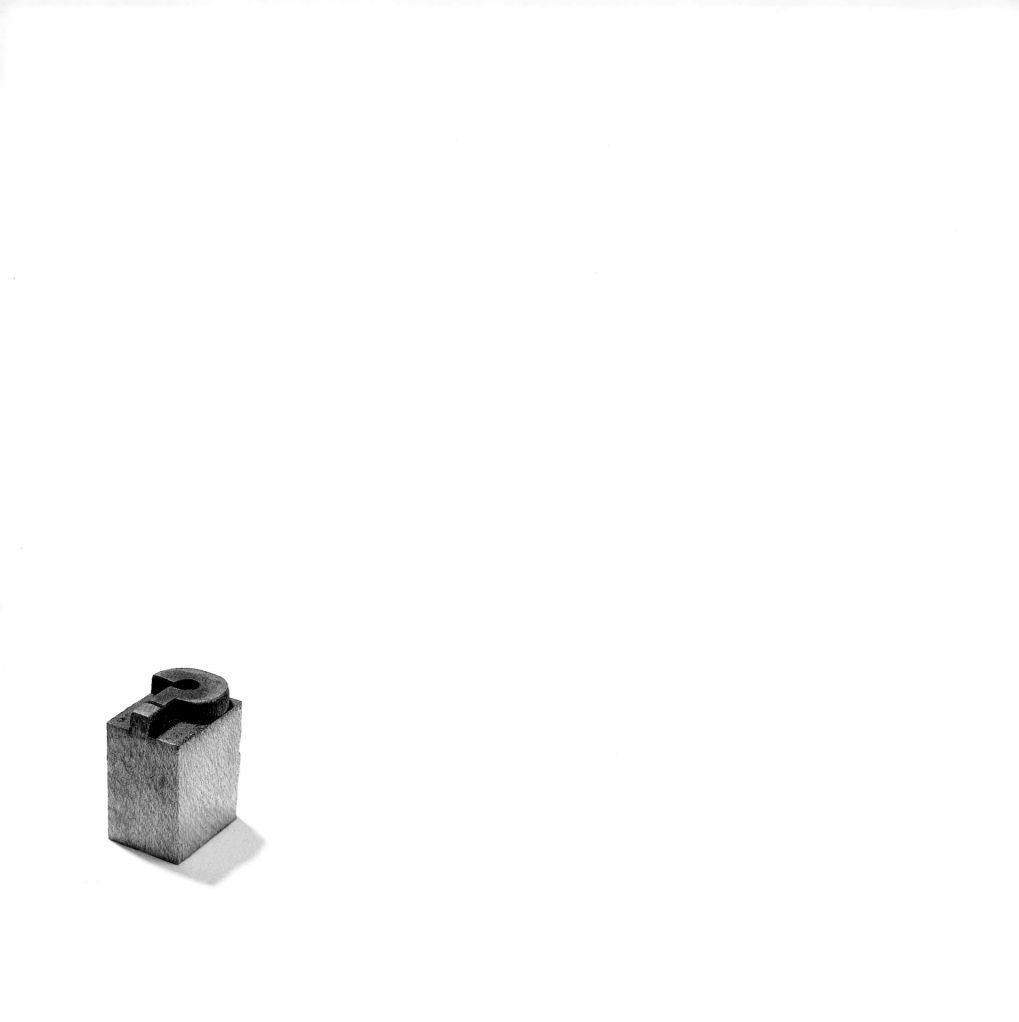

TABLE OF CONTENTS

hose who wish to govern, to make laws and impose taxes, must have access to a means of disseminating information. Until quite recently, the typographer's art and the printing press provided the only means of communication beyond word of mouth or written messages laboriously copied by hand. Therefore, a close relationship has always existed between printing and government.

In Canada in the eighteenth century,

colonial administrators, who appointed official printers to publish their laws, proclamations and notices, were the printers' most important customers. These pioneer government printers worked alone, or with the help of an apprentice or two, setting type, operating small hand presses and delivering the printed sheets. There was little bindery work, since most publications consisted of only a few loose sheets of paper.

Since then, government communications have evolved dramatically. The Queen's Printer for Canada, with approximately 25,000 book titles in print—more than any other Canadian publisher— and with more than 6,000 new releases each year, is the official publisher for Parliament, and for the departments and agencies of the federal government. With a staff of about 1,300, the Queen's Printer also oversees a broad range of government communication and advertising services; producing exhibitions, films and videos, and advising departments on their communication strategies.

But despite this greater variety of media, the need for government printing continues to increase. Today, with printing requirements worth about $200 million annually, the federal government still plays an important role in Canada's printing industry. The Queen's Printer must supply the enormous government demand for publications, as well as for other kinds of printing: the office stationery, bulletins, cheques and forms; the posters, flyers and invitations; the tickets, labels and containers; the passports; even the electoral ballots required to carry on the business of running our country.

In contrast to the simplicity of early printing, the Queen's Printer now requires about 800 employees, more than half the total staff, to look after government printing requirements alone. This group, known as Canadian Government Printing Services (CGPS), purchases about 70 percent of all printing assignments, on behalf of government departments and agencies, from commercial print shops throughout the country. The remaining 30 percent, which is too urgent or too sensitive to be submitted to the tendering process, is produced in the organization's own printing facilities, consisting of a fully equipped main plant the Printing Bureau—and a network of some 50 smaller print shops and duplicating centres located near the offices of client departments.

Today's operation is the result of a long period of evolution. The title of Queen's Printer, in its present form, dates back almost to Confederation, when the new Dominion's Parliament decided, because of cost, that government administrators would no longer appoint private printers as official printers to the Crown. Year by year, with the growth of population, transportation and commerce, and with the development of representative institutions, government printing requirements had increased correspondingly. Consequently a commission as official printer (often awarded for political reasons) represented a profitable monopoly on certain portions of the government's work.

In 1869, by the terms of "An Act respecting the Office of Queen's Printer and the Public Printing," a government official known as the Queen's Printer was appointed to supervise the printing of the Dominion's laws, of its official newspaper, the *Canada Gazette*, as well as any printing required by government departments. Although private firms would continue to execute the work under the Queen's Printer's supervision, now they were to bid for it under competitive tenders. This new arrangement, of obtaining printing under contracts on a competitive basis, was similar to the manner by which Parliament procured the printing of its own sessional records.

Despite these reforms however, the cost of printing continued to rise. With both the Queen's Printer and Parliament supervising separate sets of tenders, there was unnecessary duplication of work. At the same time, the contract system led to so many abuses that Parliament passed further legislation to reform the administration of government printing. In 1886, "An Act respecting the Department of Public Printing and Stationery" received royal assent. Under its terms, the Queen's Printer also became the Controller of Stationery, and was charged with the responsibility for all printing and binding for both Parliament and the government departments. He was made a deputy minister at the helm of the newly created Department of Public Printing and Stationery, which was to assume responsibility for all the printing previously produced by private contractors. For the first time, the Queen's Printer and Controller of Stationery was in charge of the printing for Parliament, in addition to the traditional responsibilities of printing the Dominion's laws, and the *Canada Gazette*. And, in a revolutionary departure from Canadian precedent, all this work was to be done in a printing plant directly owned and operated by the government.

However, the expectation that the new in-house printing facility would be capable of supplying all government requirements proved to be unrealistic. During the Printing Bureau's first full year in operation, the staff produced about $158,000 worth of printing, but the Queen's Printer was also obliged to pay commercial establishments about $31,000 for specialty services such as lithography and die stamping, which his own plant was not equipped to handle.

A century ago, such outside purchases amounted to less than 20 percent of the work. Today, most printing products are purchased from commercial suppliers and the ratio of outside purchases to in-house production is almost reversed. From its beginnings as a progressive nineteenth-century print shop dedicated to furnishing all government printing requirements of a general nature, the establishment has evolved into a highly specialized facility dedicated to providing a specialized range of printing services essential to the smooth functioning of Parliament and government departments.

Many of these services, such as the production of papers and reports for Parliament—delivered in both official languages, on a six-hour turn-around—are provided routinely. Others—such as the printing, collating, binding and delivery of many thousands of copies of budget documents within a few days, or of a hundred copies of briefing notes for an international summit within a few hours—can be provided on short notice, without interrupting the routine flow of parliamentary work. The Printing Bureau must be prepared to meet any government emergency, 24 hours a day, seven days a week. It is still dedicated to the unique requirements of government printing.

O f all the publications produced in Canada's national printing plant, the verbatim record of the debates of the House of Commons known as *Hansard* is perhaps the most widely recognized. *Hansard* provides a legislative history of the country, recorded in the making. It informs legislators, policy makers, diplomats and journalists, teachers and students, lawyers, historians and librarians. In a sense, *Hansard* represents all that is most important about government printing. Though we often profess to be embarrassed, amused, outraged or even disgusted by its contents, few of us would argue that a true parliamentary democracy could exist without *Hansard*'s impartial, uncensored and permanent record of its proceedings.

In Canada, the printed record appears in simultaneous, French and English editions early each morning following a parliamentary debate. This unique overnight service, producing two separate editions of *Hansard* that correspond exactly page for page, is regularly cited as the world's finest. Few people have witnessed behind-the-scenes efforts at the Queen's Printer's establishment. Here, night after night, year in and year out, people work under intense pressure in the small hours of the morning so that Canadians may read their legislators' speeches, in either of the official languages, a few hours later.

While the quality of *Hansard* printing is much higher, the pace of production equals that of any major newspaper. But unlike a newspaper, *Hansard* must take the form of two exactly matching publications despite the fact that from day to day, the printer can anticipate only roughly how large the publication will be. While Parliament usually sits from 11:00 a.m. until 6 or 6:30 p.m., the Printing Bureau must always be prepared to cope with extensions, which are frequent, and with any unusual circumstances that might generate additional work for the plant. Whether the debate is short or long, the printed *Hansard* must be ready for delivery six hours after receipt of final copy. Such a production feat, though

routine to the *Hansard* staff, would seem extraordinary to an outsider.

On the floor of the House, *Hansard* reporters for each official language replace one another every ten minutes. This means that the debates are recorded in short segments, each representing ten minutes of the proceedings. As a result, printing production of the earliest segments can often begin long before the day's debate is over. However, several hours may elapse before the House of Commons editors are ready to send final copy of even the earliest speeches to the Queen's Printer's establishment. First, each reporter who has completed a ten-minute segment must dictate all that has been said to an amanuensis, and then proofread and correct the resulting typescript. Then the editors and translators go to work on the copy. Members whose speeches are reported, and those who are referred to, are also permitted to correct any gross errors in the text—without, of course, altering its meaning.

After parliamentary speeches are recorded and transcribed, they are translated into the other official language. Since translations must also be corrected to reflect editorial revisions made to the originals, translated copy normally does not begin to arrive at the Bureau until the entire original text for the debate has become available. Typically the bulk of *Hansard* copy arrives at the printer's towards the end of the night.

The work of the reporters, seated at their desks in the middle of the Chamber's centre aisle, recording with intense concentration, is the only public evidence of *Hansard* in the making. But until recently, another sign was a small green van that left Parliament Hill several times each day that the House was in session and disappeared down Wellington Street towards its destination: the Queen's Printer's Main Plant in Hull. There, a uniformed messenger carrying a slim envelope jumped from the vehicle and hurried inside. In the envelope were a few pages of rough typescript for the nation's daily *Hansard*.

This journey formed part of a 100-year-old ritual that the computer has finally rendered obsolete. Since 1986, the bits and pieces of *Hansard* typescript that used to be rushed to the Queen's Printer's as quickly as they became available, by messengers who walked or bicycled, and later drove motorized vehicles, are now communicated on-line to the Main Plant's computer. Because of its complex production routine, *Hansard* was last of all parliamentary publications to be transmitted in this manner. And one of the last sessions for which the Printing Bureau produced *Hansard* in the traditional way took place on February 4, 1986.

That day's debate generated a typical night's work at the Printing Bureau. As usual, the House convened at 11:00 a.m. Production began at the Queen's Printer's at 4:20 p.m., when a messenger arrived with the first 47 pages—printers call them "folios"—of *Hansard* typescript. Further deliveries followed in rapid succession, but when the House adjourned at 6:31 p.m., the printer had less than one third of the debate in English-language typescript. By 10:05 p.m. all 437 folios of the English copy were at the Main Plant. However, half of these arrived in the

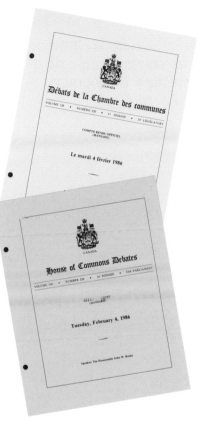

last 45 minutes. The bulk of French-language text, which usually requires much more translation, arrived even later—more than half of it between midnight and 2:30 a.m., when the last 49 folios were logged in. Six hours later, at 8:30 a.m., printed and finished *Hansard* booklets were loaded onto a van for delivery to the House of Commons, and the offices of the Prime Minister and the Privy Council.

How was this production miracle accomplished? The process began in the composing room, with a staff of approximately nine bilingual workers in the evening, and fourteen at night. Their exact starting time depends upon the quantity of text received, how long the House is expected to sit, and how much other parliamentary work has to be produced during the night. On February 4, production began with 153 English folios, at 7:30 p.m. Beginning the job too soon, with too little available text, might have resulted in later scheduling conflicts with other jobs. Starting too late might have meant not getting the work completed on time.

11:00 a.m.

11:30 a.m.

7:30 p.m.

4:20 p.m.

11:00 a.m.
In the House of Commons, *Hansard* reporters create a verbatim record of the proceedings.

11:30 a.m.
Debates Reporter Joan Henderson checks the typescript of her notes.

4:20 p.m.
At the Queen's Printer's Main Plant, Robert Tessier accepts a delivery of rough *Hansard* typescript from House of Commons Messenger Robert Séguin.

7:30 p.m.
Suzanne Bériault begins coding the rough typescript with instructions for the computer.

As the first step, copy mark-up people divided the 153 folios into production units of two to three double-spaced, typewritten pages each, referred to as "takes." About three takes comprise a single page of *Hansard* after the copy is set up in columns and reduced to *Hansard*'s smaller type size. Since copy does not necessarily arrive in its correct order, space allowance must be made for missing text, particularly for translated portions, which are inserted as they become available. Each take has to be marked with the necessary instructions to the computer.

Within minutes, terminal operators could begin inputting the first takes. These operators try to maintain a pace of 10,000 keystrokes an hour, even when typescripts contain numerous handwritten notes and corrections. Tables and other complex materials are assembled on a separate photocomposition system with its own mini-computer, and later stripped into the text by hand.

A printout generated from each take, referred to as a "galley," was sent to the proofroom along with the typescript. Here proofreaders checked the galleys, not merely for accuracy to copy, but also for such things as style, typographical errors and formatting codes. Depending on their workload and the number of errors, proofreaders either make the corrections themselves at their terminals or return marked copy to the terminal operators.

Camera-ready copy can be generated from the galleys only after all missing items, such as the translated portions, become available to fill any gaps in the text sequence. On February 4, half of the English-language typescript arrived at the plant only a short time before the final delivery at 10:05 p.m., so it was 12:55 a.m. before the proofreaders could complete a sequence of English-language galleys and send for the first batch of camera-ready copy from the computer.

Twenty minutes later, at 1:15 a.m., the text arrived in the proofroom, photocomposed into 16 pages arranged exactly as they would appear in the printed version of *Hansard*. Here, proofreaders checked the camera-ready copy again, and also ensured that the English and French versions were exactly balanced, paragraph for paragraph. This balancing is required to produce the *Hansard* index at the end of the month.

From this point, any further revisions or other unforeseen corrections from the House of Commons have to be photocomposed separately, as is tabular matter, and manually stripped, line by line, into the camera-ready pages. Fortunately, on February 4, no such alterations were required.

In the computer room, a staff of three people on each shift can fill an order for camera-ready copy in as little as 13 minutes. The computer-driven typesetter generates photocomposed pages from transmitted data. At the same time, the data is stored on a tape, created for archival purposes. In case of an on-line power breakdown such tapes can serve as back-up. Stored in the Main Plant's tape archive, they can be corrected, and are used later, to reproduce camera-ready copy for *Hansard*'s revised edition.

Though fire, flood or strike might hinder the Queen's Printer in the performance of his duties, little

7:35 p.m.

7:45 p.m.

7:35 p.m.
Typesetting machine operators Lucille Benoit and her daughter, Nicole, start to input text and formatting codes. Looking on is Pierre Gravel.

7:45 p.m.
Proofreader Marcel Huot checks computer printouts, or galleys, for accuracy and agreement with the original typescript.

12:55 a.m.
Hélène Grabst operates a computer-driven typesetter. In the foreground is the back-up tape, which is generated simultaneously with the camera-ready copy.

1:15 a.m.
As camera-ready copy emerges from the computer-driven typesetter, it is returned to the proofroom, where it will be checked again.

1:15 a.m.

12:55 a.m.

else, such as equipment and power failures, would relieve him of his responsibilities to Canada's Parliament. For each piece of equipment in the Main Plant, there is another ready to serve as emergency back-up. There is a fully equipped in-house machine shop, with machinists and electronic technicians on duty or on call 24 hours a day, seven days a week.

In case of an interruption or fluctuation in power, a back-up electrical system smoothes voltage irregularities and supplies power for up to 15 minutes, until the essential services can be switched to emergency generators. Without this system the computer operation would be particularly vulnerable. An interruption, or even a fluctuation in power lasting only a fraction of a second, could cause the entire system to lose any text not already in storage.

The equipment steadily generates camera-ready copy as soon as the go-ahead is received. On this night, the last batch of English-language copy was returned to the proofroom at 2:30 a.m., just as the final 49 pages of French-language typescript arrived at the Main Plant's front door. Three hours later, at 5:29 a.m., computer-room staff completed the last batch of camera-ready French text and finished their portion of the night's work. Once pages had passed final inspection by the proofreaders, they were ready for the offset printing process.

Offset preparation includes all the steps necessary to reproduce camera-ready copy onto large printing plates that will be mounted on the press. First, the pages must be photographed, or "imposed," on large negatives from which the printing plates will be processed. At this stage, the copy cannot be left in the sequence in which it will appear in print. Instead, pages must be divided into groups that conveniently fit the large sheets of printing paper stock used on the press, and arranged in such a way that, when the large sheets are folded and trimmed after printing, the pages will once again follow one another in correct numerical order.

Printers refer to such a group of pages folded together as a "signature." The order in which the pages must appear on the negatives is governed by the method in which the signatures will be bound into a publication in the bindery. Many different page configurations are possible. *Hansard* is printed in 32-page signatures, each signature consisting of two large printed sheets folded together. Except when the publication is too large, running to more than three signatures, or 96 pages, *Hansard* is finished on the saddle-wire binding machine. This machine stitches signatures through their centres with wire staples, fastening them together into pamphlets. In any pamphlet stitched this way (through its centre), the first and last pages are "companion pages," printed side by side on a single sheet of paper. The second page's companion is the second to last page, and so on. Consequently, before even one signature can be prepared for offset printing, the first and last pages must be available, which usually means that the entire publication must be ready before offset preparation work can begin.

Once all the camera-ready copy is available, the staff (four on the evening shift and about eleven on

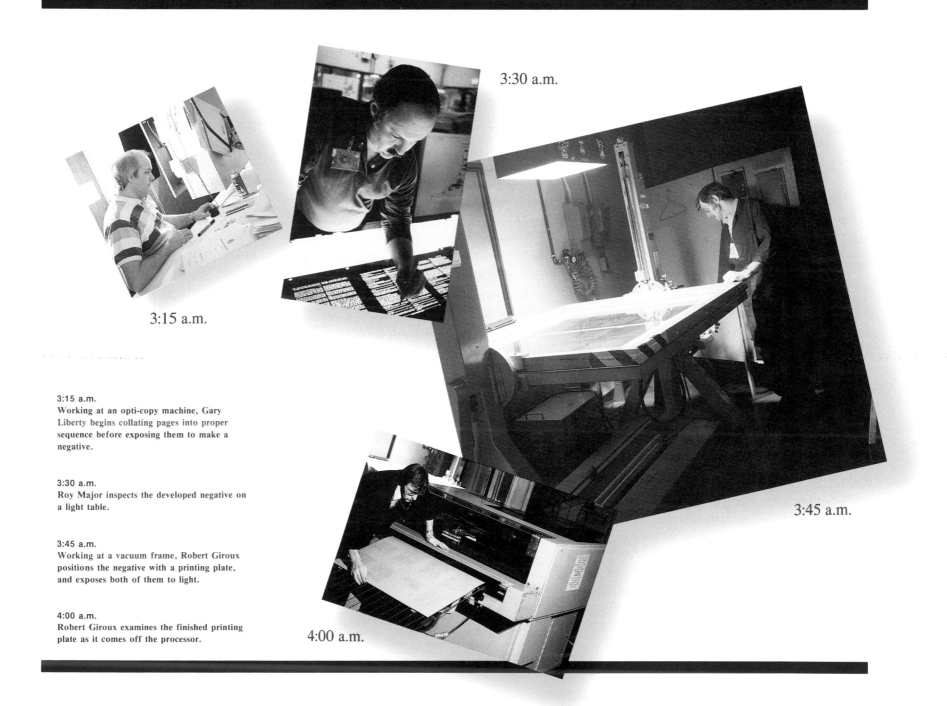

3:30 a.m.

3:15 a.m.

3:45 a.m.

4:00 a.m.

3:15 a.m.
Working at an opti-copy machine, Gary
Liberty begins collating pages into proper
sequence before exposing them to make a
negative.

3:30 a.m.
Roy Major inspects the developed negative on
a light table.

3:45 a.m.
Working at a vacuum frame, Robert Giroux
positions the negative with a printing plate,
and exposes both of them to light.

4:00 a.m.
Robert Giroux examines the finished printing
plate as it comes off the processor.

16

the night shift) can prepare an entire *Hansard* for press in just under one hour. Their task is made considerably faster by the use of a fully automatic camera, which they can program to impose pages in correct sequence on film to create a signature. If the pages arrive late enough to make it necessary, up to three people can operate this equipment. One person works the camera; another collates pages into proper sequence and punches holes in the paper to position it correctly on the board from which the exposure will be made; a third person may be in the darkroom preparing film and feeding the film processor.

Each developed negative, called a "layout," must be inspected on a light table. Tiny flaws, such as pinholes of light, are opaqued before the negatives are numbered and keyed for correct positioning on the printing plate. Four 8-page plates are required to print each of *Hansard*'s 32-page signatures. Even at this late stage, an error may be discovered. Then the faulty page must be photographed again and manually stripped into the layout.

Finally, the developed negative is positioned on a presensitized aluminum printing plate, placed in a vacuum frame, and exposed to a metal halide light. Light passing through the image areas, which are clear on the negative, exposes the image onto the surface of the plate. From the vacuum frame, the exposed plate is quickly passed through a plate processor, where a developing solution is applied. The developer cleans the unexposed, non-image areas of the plate. The exposed image areas, which have been hardened by light, remain sensitized. They are grease or ink

receptive, while the rest of the plate is not. The developed plate, like a developed photograph, is no longer sensitive to light. Hence, the image remains fixed on the plate.

In the processor, the printing plate is also rinsed, and a gum is applied to prevent surface scratches and oxidation. The plate then passes through a heat dryer and is ready for the press. Once the protective gum is removed for printing, water is repelled from the image areas of the plate, which are grease receptive. As a result, the printing ink, which is greasy, is trapped wherever an image is to appear.

The February 4 issue consisted of two signatures, or 64 pages, in each language. The offset preparation staff received camera-ready copy for the entire English-language publication at 3:15 a.m. By 5:05 a.m. they had delivered all the printing plates for both signatures of the English-language *Hansard* to the pressroom. French-language camera copy was not ready for offset preparation until 6:10 and 6:20 a.m. The resulting plates went to press at 7:10 and at 7:20 a.m., just over an hour before delivery time.

By the time the pressroom received the last signature for the French edition, only a few precious minutes remained before the delivery deadline. The two web offset presses available for *Hansard* print 32 pages in one pass, and automatically fold the sheets into signatures ready for binding. On this night, to finish in time, both presses had to run simultaneously.

At 7:20 on the morning of February 5, the plates for the second French signature arrived in the pressroom. The 6,200 English copies of *Hansard* were

5:05 a.m.

7:45 a.m.

8:30 a.m.

5:05 a.m.
Maurice Lamirande checks the quality of printed signatures as they begin to roll off the press.

7:45 a.m.
In the bindery, Simone Jean loads the first French-language signatures onto the saddle-wire binding machine, where they are stitched into booklets.

8:30 a.m.
Queen's Printer Norman Manchevsky reviews an early morning copy of yesterday's debate.

For an average night's production, the Main Plant consumes about 4 rolls, or 5,200 pounds of paper.

already finished in the bindery, and the 800 English copies required for the House of Commons, and for the offices of the Prime Minister and the Privy Council—called "pre-advance" copies—were on the loading dock ready for delivery. The full run of 2,450 copies of the French version of *Hansard* did not come off the press until 8:25 a.m., too late to be delivered by 8:30. Consequently, the first 245 copies of the last French signature—the number required to make up the pre-advance edition—were rushed to the bindery at 7:45 a.m.

Working at the feeding end of the saddle-wire binding machine, some of the bindery staff quickly loaded the pre-advance signatures. Others removed finished pamphlets from the delivery end and rushed them to a drilling machine where they were punched with holes for insertion into three-ring binders. The first 245 copies of the French-language *Hansard* were then rushed out to the loading dock.

It was 8:30 a.m., precisely six hours after the final batch of rough copy had been delivered earlier that morning. The staff loaded the delivery truck with the copies of *Hansard* destined for Parliament Hill. Other advance deliveries followed shortly, and later that day the remaining copies were in the mail.

The *Hansard* that we have been following was not that night's only production achievement. The Queen's Printer is also responsible for all other parliamentary papers and publications, each with its own stringent production deadline. On the night of February 4, the Printing Bureau also produced *Votes and Proceedings* and *Orders of the Day* for the House of Commons; *Debates* and *Minutes* for the Senate; various parliamentary committee reports; and 157 pages of other miscellaneous printing—a typical night's work during the parliamentary session.

*. . . a Printer is indispensibly necessary; and tho'
many may be found to rush into crowded cities,
I see no likelihood that any Person will venture
into a Wilderness and yet in the Infancy of this
Establishment He will be found to be of the
utmost Utility.*

Lieutenant-Governor John Graves Simcoe,
writing to the Secretary of State
Home Affairs, about organizing government
in Upper Canada, 1791

Prior to the intro-duction of the first printing press to the territory that would later become Canada, administrators had to rely on the traditional town crier and public readings to communicate with the populace. Under those circumstances, it is not surprising that they quickly recognized the advantages of publishing their laws, and of printing their announcements as proclamations and notices in semi-official newspapers or "gazettes." Consequently, early printing presses were often established under the auspices of government, or at least in response to government requirements rather than to popular demand.

By the same token, their association with government was important to pioneer printers, who were usually able to subsist only through whatever official patronage they received. The isolated little settlements of the colonies provided few potential newspaper subscribers, and little news to print. Original material could easily be a source of displeasure to the local authorities, and news reprinted from American and European newspapers could be many months old before copies reached the settlement. Sometimes the Church or individuals provided material to feed a press, but official notices, proclamations and laws formed the early printers' mainstay.

This was certainly true for Canada's first newspaper and job printing business, established in Halifax in 1752. Its press, also Canada's first, was brought from Boston by Bartholomew Green, Jr., member of a family of famous printers who were responsible for printing the first newspaper on this continent in 1704. Green arrived in Halifax in August 1751 but died only a few weeks later without having had a chance to do any printing. The distinction of being Canada's first printer went instead to John Bushell, who followed Green from Boston to Halifax and in 1752 issued *The Halifax Gazette*, the first newspaper and first known printing in Canada.

By today's standards, it was not much of a newspaper, just half a sheet of foolscap printed on both sides. Halifax itself had just been established and was a mere garrison. Besides the official notices, Bushell had little news to print, and circulation of his newspaper was almost entirely limited to the tiny town. However, he was a skillful printer, according to Isaiah Thomas, the historian of American printing who was apprenticed for a while to Bushell's successor, Anton Heinrich.

Heinrich, who acquired Bushell's print shop in 1761, was an astute businessman. He was also one of the most colourful personalities in the history of Maritime printing. To edit and publish his newspaper, Heinrich translated his name to Anthony Henry. Under his original name, Anton Heinrich, he printed another paper in German for settlers in Lunenburg. Isaiah Thomas, Henry's apprentice, tells us that, unlike his predecessor, Henry sometimes printed "in a very indifferent manner"; nevertheless, his Halifax paper became what some historians have called the liveliest journal of opinion of the century in Canada. Henry enjoyed a long and fruitful career of over 40 years, even surviving a dispute with the Nova Scotia authorities that cost him the official patronage. Through his own persistence, Henry was eventually reinstated as government printer, and in 1788 he was officially named King's Printer for Nova Scotia.

According to most historians, during Bushell and Henry's early years there was no printing press in New France. In 1763, under the terms of the Treaty of Paris, the British acquired sovereignty over the territory of Quebec and established government by Governor in Council. Shortly after the treaty was signed, two Scottish printers from Philadelphia appeared in the town of Quebec. William Brown and Thomas Gilmore had gone into partnership in Philadelphia. Before joining his partner in Quebec, Gilmore went to England to purchase a font of type, a press and printing paper. The printers' arrival was fortunate for the first British governor, James Murray, because the change from French to British administration required many new edicts and proclamations. The political situation in turn helped the printers, since the Governor in Council was quick to make use of their new printing office. In 1766, Brown and Gilmore were jointly appointed official printer to His Majesty.

Besides being Quebec's first printers and its first government printers, Brown and Gilmore were also responsible for another important "first": they were the founders of bilingual publishing in Canada. Having attracted fewer than 150 subscribers to their

newspaper, about half English, half French-speaking, the printers announced in their first issue, on June 21, 1764, "Our design therefore is to publish in English and French, under the title of *The Quebec Gazette.*"

Their experiment proved to be a success. At first, the paper was a semi-official one, with government proclamations run off as special supplements. Later, when the printers became less dependent on government support, the publication gained a reputation for unrestrained discussion of contentious issues and events.

Brown, always the senior partner, continued alone in the business after Gilmore's death in 1772. As a printer, Brown maintained very high technical standards, producing many works that historians of printing have compared favourably with anything printed in North America or Europe at the time. He issued some 250 separate publications, though fewer than ten ran to more than 100 pages. Just as *The*

Canada's First Government Printer

During his ten years in Halifax, John Bushell was in debt more often than not. The tiny subscription list and slim advertising revenue of *The Halifax Gazette* could not sustain him. Bushell's press, like other early print shops, depended for its survival on official printing jobs for the government of Nova Scotia, which provided a regular, if small income. Besides, the printer suffered from a personal shortcoming that added greatly to his problem.

Bushell was prosecuted for debt several times, often for unpaid grocer's bills, on which debits for liquid, rather than solid sustenance, predominated. His love of the bottle got him into trouble with the authorities so often that it has become a matter of historic record. Isaiah Thomas said, "Bushell had not the art of acquiring property nor did he make the most economical use of the little which fell into his hands."

Bushell's debut as a government printer, and the beginning of official printing in Canada, is thought to have been a small pamphlet in which was printed a 1752 law entitled, "An Act for the Relief of Debtors, with respect to the Imprisonment of their Persons," a somewhat ironic subject considering the printer's own frailties. Nonetheless, the pamphlet is a fine example of the typographer's art and was set by an excellent craftsman, or craftswoman (Bushell's daughter Elizabeth is supposed to have been an excellent compositor).

The Bushells went on to do much more government printing. Elizabeth Bushell's brother was also a trained printer, but neither of Bushell's children continued the business after their father's death in 1761.

The first invoice that William Brown and Thomas Gilmore, Quebec's first printers, submitted to the civil government established in August 1764. It shows some of the earliest proclamations and ordinances promulgated by the new administration.

Quebec Gazette/La Gazette de Québec provides an historical record of contemporary life and opinion, Brown and Gilmore's official documents chronicle the major political developments of their time.

When Brown died in 1789, the print shop passed to Samuel Neilson, his nephew from Scotland, whose family continued running it until the middle of the nineteenth century. The little shop gradually grew into a large printing office, reputedly the centre of printing in Canada for almost half a century.

One of Brown's typographic masterpieces was the Quebec Act, which he printed in bilingual format in 1774. The Act was passed by the British Parliament in response to colonial dissatisfaction with the system of government. Unfortunately, however, its typography was much more attractive than its terms, which were that a governor would continue to rule with the help of a council, whose members were appointed by the King. There was to be no government by represen-tation, since the Act stipulated that a general assembly was not to be convened.

Meanwhile, as a result of the American Revolution, loyal British subjects began settling in large numbers in western parts of Quebec. These people were accustomed to a representative government and were unwilling to be governed solely by a governor and his council sitting at the capital. In 1791, partly to resolve their concerns and partly to encourage further Loyalist settlement, the British Parliament passed further legislation. The Constitution Act divided Quebec into two provinces, called Upper and Lower Canada, and established for each a system of representative government. In each province, a governor and his legislative council, appointed at the Crown's pleasure, were to share political power with a people's assembly, elected by property owners.

The Constitution Act was printed by William Moore. This printer, who first appeared in Quebec

---

The Quebec Gazette and the Stamp Act

Brown and Gilmore's *The Quebec Gazette/La Gazette de Québec* remained in publication for over 100 years, with only two short interruptions. One was caused by the hated Stamp Act, which was passed in Britain in 1765. The Act imposed a duty on all paper used in the colonies, and declared all writings on unstamped paper to be illegal. Seriously opposed in the 13 colonies to the south, the Act was one of the inciting causes of the American Revolution. In Quebec, it raised the cost of *The Quebec Gazette* by

about a penny an issue to a price many of its subscribers could not afford, and forced the printers to suspend publication for a short time. A few months later, after the Stamp Act was repealed, *The Gazette* called the Act "more dreadful than the icy chains of our inhospitable winter whose harmful blasts spread desolation over the plains and stop the source of commerce." Nevertheless, it also generated some income, for in 1766, Brown and Gilmore printed 400 copies of the Stamp Act in French.

Early Printing in Upper Canada

Producing a printed document was a slow process that required considerable skill as well as muscle power. First, written matter had to be converted by hand into lines of type suitable for printing on the screw press. Each line was assembled in a composing stick, letter by letter, and justified by inserting metal blanks to make lines of equal length. Once proofs were pulled, and errors corrected, the type was made up into pages and firmly locked in a metal frame that could be carried to the press for printing.

The locked-up type was laid on the solid plate, called the press "bed," and daubed with ink. A sheet of dampened paper was placed on the tympan (shown in raised position), and a crank was turned to position the bed, type and tympan directly underneath the heavy block, or "platen." The platen was attached to the base of an iron spindle or screw. By pulling the bar, the spindle was turned, and the platen forced down hard enough to squeeze the paper against the type. Then the platen was screwed up again, so the printed sheet could be pulled away and hung up to dry.

Presswork was hazardous, and far more laborious than typesetting, because great pressure was required from the screw and platen upon type and paper to make the impression. Usually the work was shared between two people — one pulling, while the other, often an apprentice, inked the type — producing printed sheets at a rate of about 60 an hour.

Printers have traditionally identified this wooden screw-press as the one that Lieutenant-Governor Simcoe and his printer, Louis Roy, brought to Newark to establish the first printing office in Upper Canada. Built in England, the press was supposed to have been imported by William Brown, and sold a few years later by his successors, the Neilsons, to Louis Roy. After Roy left Upper Canada in 1794, it continued to be used for many years by successive government printers. The press, which is now in the National Museum of Science and Technology, is typical of presses used by early Canadian printers.

as the head of a company of actors, established a Nouvelle Imprimerie as a rival to Brown's business in 1786, but soon lost his printing equipment to the bailiff. John Jones acquired the printing office at the sale, and in less than a year sold it to William Vondenvelden, his printer. In August 1795, Vondenvelden was officially appointed first Law Printer to the new administration of Lower Canada.

The creation of Upper Canada led directly to the establishment of the province's first printing press. The task of organizing society and government in what was still a wilderness fell to its first lieutenant-governor, John Graves Simcoe. To promote settlement, communications and trade in the interests of King George III, a printer was "indispensably necessary," according to the newly appointed Simcoe.

On his way to Upper Canada, Simcoe stopped in Quebec, where Samuel Neilson recommended a printer willing to go with him. This was Louis Roy, who set up the province's first printing press. In September 1792, the Lieutenant-Governor and his new printer arrived in Newark (now Niagara-on-the-Lake), the newly selected capital in the heart of Loyalist settlement. En route, Simcoe had been obliged to ask Montreal printer Fleury Mesplet to print some proclamations for him, and was incensed to find that Mesplet had called himself "King's Printer." "His Excellency wishes to know under what authority you consider yourself the Government Printer of this Province," scolded Simcoe's assistant. "Mr. Louis Roy has long been officiating as Printer of Upper Canada, and while he continues to perform the duty

with punctuality and satisfaction he will not, of course, be superseded."

In November 1792, the government of Upper Canada ordered printing paper and a variety of typefaces from England. The order was a large one for those days. It included roman and italic typefaces in many sizes—brevier, long primer, small pica, pica, great primer and double pica—all needed for printing newspapers, pamphlets and various other publications. The first issue of Roy's *Upper Canada Gazette* appeared in April 1793. It was a semi-official vehicle which the printer was free to fill up as he pleased after printing the official announcements.

Before the end of 1794, Roy resigned his position and returned to Montreal. Whether it was because he had ceased to perform with "satisfaction"—Mrs. Simcoe complained that Roy could not write good English—or because he was fed up with the terms of his employment, is not known. Whatever the reasons were, his employer was a hard taskmaster. After Roy's departure, the administration appointed and dismissed eight more King's Printers in rapid succession, often for political reasons. Only Robert Stanton, tenth and last King's Printer to Upper Canada, kept his job for more than a few years. Stanton was appointed in 1826, and continued to print the government's laws and *Upper Canada Gazette* until 1841, when new legislation made his position uncertain.

That year, the Union Act, which re-united the provinces of Upper and Lower Canada under one administration, came into force. It bears the imprint of two men: Stewart Derbishire, the Provincial Assembly's Member for Bytown (Ottawa) and George Desbarats, printer of *The Quebec Mercury*, an official government vehicle. Though the Union Act embodied Lord Durham's recommendation for responsible government for the new United Province of Canada, it was through the courtesy of the new governor, not the Province's elected assembly, that Derbishire and Desbarats were appointed "to be jointly our Printer and Law Printer in and for our Province of Canada" on September 29, 1841. With each of them retaining his title until death, Derbishire

and Desbarats would dominate government printing for nearly a quarter century, until shortly before Confederation.

There were many others who had had their hearts set on becoming Queen's Printer (Queen Victoria began her reign in 1837), and outcries were heard from all. Their chief target, probably because he was neither a printer nor a Canadian, was Stewart Derbishire. Of all the complaints, perhaps the most understandable were those which came from the official printers for the former administrations of Upper and Lower Canada. Since the Union

George-Paschal Desbarats: A Family Dynasty

When provincial administrators appointed George-Paschal Desbarats Queen's Printer, they chose a man whose family had been involved in government printing for nearly 200 years, first in France and more recently in Canada.

The first printer in the family was Pierre Desbarats, who in 1651 established the first printing office in Pau, a small city near the Pyrenees in France. He was succeeded by other generations of Desbarats printers, including a great-granddaughter, Jeanne Desbarats who had her printing office closed and her presses and type sold because women were not permitted to operate such businesses.

Soon after the last Desbarats to serve as royal printer in France died, other members of the family began to play an

George-Paschal Desbarats
Her Majesty's Printer and Law Printer 1841-1864

important role in government printing in the New World. In 1798, George-Paschal's father, Pierre-Édouard, became a Law Printer in Lower Canada.

Pierre-Édouard had entered government service as a translator for the Legislative Council, and had become Assistant Clerk of the Legislative Assembly. In partnership with Roger Lelièvre, he purchased Quebec's Nouvelle Imprimerie from William Vondenvelden. In 1798, Desbarats and Lelièvre succeeded Vondenvelden jointly as Law Printer, but Desbarats soon bought out his partner, and in 1800, became sole Law Printer for the Province of Lower Canada, a position he held until his death in April 1828.

Pierre-Édouard had nine children; third among them was George-Paschal, born August 11, 1808. This son at first pursued other interests and became involved in the government's new patent entitled the bearers to work previously done by official printers for both former provinces, an obvious arrangement would have been to appoint the official printers for Upper and Lower Canada jointly as Her Majesty's Printer for the United Province of Canada. Yet, the incumbents to those positions were passed over.

Robert Stanton, the Queen's Printer for Upper Canada, was particularly upset because Sydenham, the new governor, had promised that he would be considered for the post. In Lower Canada, John Charlton Fisher and William Kemble had been joint King's Printer since 1826, and joint Law Printer since 1828. Section 47 of the Union Act stipulated that commissions and appointments in effect under the former provinces would continue under the new legislation, unless changed by an act of the legislature of the Province of Canada. Basing their claim on this clause, Stanton, Fisher and Kemble petitioned the government in 1841. They wanted Desbarats and Derbishire's patent repealed; failing that, they demanded compensation for lost profits.

Their requests were refused, but the petitions were not entirely unsuccessful. Sydenham's successor,

family's printing business only after his father became ill in 1826.

The family business, already a thriving enterprise, continued to prosper under George-Paschal's direction. At first, the new proprietor was associated with Thomas Cary, publisher of *The Quebec Mercury*; their joint imprint appears on various government documents. One of their last joint ventures was the printing for the Provincial Assembly's first session, executed just prior to George-Paschal's appointment as Queen's Printer.

George-Paschal Desbarats was an astute and successful businessman, with many interests besides printing. Over the years, he invested the healthy profits generated by his commission to build the Desbarats fortune in earnest. At the same time, he used his wealth to help develop the country's resources. In 1847, Desbarats and Stewart

Derbishire invested in the province's first glass factory, newly established just west of Montreal. He also put money into one of the earliest railway lines, and wrote a pamphlet on its behalf. Diversifying further, George-Paschal bought large amounts of land, including extensive tracts being developed for mining. One such property on the north shore of Lake Huron is now the site of Desbarats, Ontario.

Despite his many other involvements, George-Paschal retained his love for the printing business throughout his life. He was exceedingly proud of the Queen's print shop, as he had made and managed it. After his death the *Montreal Gazette* recalled: "It used to be his boast that he had the best printers that could be procured and that nothing sent to his office in confidence ever reached the public through any of his employees."

George-Paschal retained the commission for government printing until his death in November 1864. The family tradition of government printing was carried on by his oldest child, George Edward, who later was appointed first Queen's Printer for the Dominion of Canada.

This volume was printed in bilingual format by George-Paschal's father, Pierre-Édouard Desbarats.

Stewart Derbishire

It would be difficult to conceive of a more unlikely partner for George-Paschal Desbarats than fellow Queen's Printer Stewart Derbishire. Yet Derbishire, a flamboyant adventurer who enjoyed the reputation of an advanced liberal, was in many ways a perfect foil to the correct and conservative Desbarats. Unlike Desbarats, a third generation Canadian with cultural roots sunk deeply into both French and English Canada, Derbishire had been in North America barely three years when his appointment was made.

A doctor's son from England, and a man of pronounced opinions and enormous enthusiasm, Derbishire began a military career but soon switched to the study of law. As a lawyer, he was involved in several cases of great public interest; particularly noted was his spirited defense of some disgruntled Dorchester labourers prosecuted for destroying machinery in 1832. Despite a growing reputation, however, Derbishire soon relinquished his legal career, and became a crusading political journalist. He also became interested in the civil war in Spain, where a British contingent fought on the side of Queen Isabella. Sent there as a newspaper correspondent in 1837, he immediately volunteered for service and, after a brief involvement in a number of military campaigns, was decorated for gallantry.

Derbishire had returned to England and was publishing a newspaper when he heard of Lord Durham's mission to Canada. In January 1838, supposing that the rebellions in Canada would provide an opportunity for him to participate in another adventure, Derbishire wrote to Lord Durham. His experience as a lawyer, political journalist and soldier, he suggested,

Stewart Derbishire
Her Majesty's Printer and Law Printer 1841–1863

particularly suited him for "employment in Canada where Civil Society is exposed to military surprises and where the safety of the State may depend upon the aptitude of civilians to take a soldier's part upon emergencies." Lord Durham agreed. A few months later, Derbishire was on confidential assignment for His Lordship.

In New York State, Derbishire won interviews with William Lyon Mackenzie and other rebel leaders in exile, and obtained information about their views and activities. In Montreal, he visited Denis-Benjamin Viger, and spoke with many other *Canadiens* who had suffered during the rebellion. Derbishire's observations, embodied in a report to Lord Durham, demonstrate that he had inspired confidence in those he interviewed. Unlike Lord Durham, Derbishire considered French Canada entirely irreconcilable to the existing system and warned that the rebellion was by no means over. Contemporary biographers even claim he made Canada his home partially "to see the fun" of another uprising, which he believed to be imminent.

During the course of his diplomatic duties, Derbishire is supposed to have brought Durham the news that Britain refused Durham's bid to grant amnesty to the rebels. Derbishire correctly predicted that his news would "make his lordship kick and throw up his commission." Shortly after Durham's departure in 1838, when rebellion again flared up, Derbishire made a midwinter dash to Fredericton and Halifax, at some risk to his life, to summon reinforcements.

It was his last involvement in soldiering. By 1840, after spending some time in the United States on special assignment to the British government, Derbishire was back in Montreal, editing *The Morning Courier*, an official government vehicle. Now wishing to be considered "discreetly liberal,"

Governor Metcalfe, conceded that "an act of injustice was committed when those officers were deprived of the advantages of which they were in possession, without reason assigned, by a mere act of authority, in order to transfer those advantages to more favoured individuals." Stanton was permitted to continue publishing the *Upper Canada Gazette* for almost two years, and in March 1845, Fisher was given a minor appointment as Printer to Her Majesty within Lower Canada.

Apart from these concessions, however, the government of the United Canadas abandoned the former patent holders. But in other ways its printing arrangements were based on the tradition of government printing that had grown in Upper and Lower Canada since Brown and Gilmore were first commissioned to print the government's legal notices in *The Quebec Gazette*. This tradition, only partially reflected in legislation, defined the role of the Queen's Printer.

The new administration continued the policy whereby Her Majesty's Printer and Law Printer was responsible for printing and distributing the laws each session, and the official government newspaper each week. Consequently, under their commission, Desbarats and Derbishire were responsible for printing the *Statutes* and the *Canada Gazette*. In 1845, an act was passed requiring the Queen's Printer to submit annual reports on the distribution of the *Statutes*. In 1849, the Interpretation Act also enshrined in law the tradition that the Queen's Printer was responsible for the accuracy of the laws he promulgated. Section 27 of the Act declared that the Queen's Printer's imprint would constitute legal proof of an act's authenticity.

Derbishire soon re-established close ties with government, particularly with the new governor, Lord Sydenham.

In 1841, thanks to Sydenham's personal intervention, Derbishire became the Provincial Assembly's first member for Bytown. His position created much resentment, for he had had little to do with the place. His appointment as Queen's Printer with Desbarats later that year was also the direct result of Sydenham's patronage. According to Derbishire, it was a "fancy" of Lord Sydenham's that "a lawyer should always be in the Commission here and at home." This appointment was followed by another round of scathing attacks on Derbishire. Resentment over executive interference went so far, he said, that "all the efforts of party here and at home were made to get my appointment disallowed. It would take me a week to tell you what was done." But the attacks against him were unsuccessful: Derbishire retained the Queen's Printer's commission for the rest of his life. However, the Bytown seat he soon relinquished, for another reason. In 1844, "An Act for better securing the Independence of the Legislative Assembly of this Province" prohibited the Queen's Printer from sitting in Parliament.

Despite a healthy income from the commission, Derbishire lacked his partner's interest in the acquisition of property. In Canada he was known for his generosity, and for his lavish spending so people "might know that it was not riches he sought in making Canada his home."

Being unfamiliar with printing, Derbishire probably had little to do with the day-to-day operation of the Queen's Printer's establishment. However, he had other talents to contribute. It was usually Derbishire, not Desbarats, who appeared at various times before the Joint Committee on Printing, and whose skillful responses to embarrassing questions went some way towards ensuring the partnership's long-term success.

. . . I am in the Commission for printing the
Laws . . . . They say it is to be lucrative. I shall
not object if it should turn out to be so.

Stewart Derbishire, 1841

n 1841, Derbishire wrote that he expected his appointment to be a lucrative one, and his expectation was not disappointed. As holder of letters made patent, the Queen's Printer enjoyed a monopoly and was not required to tender in competition with other print shops. Desbarats and Derbishire, like their predecessors, were paid at fixed rates determined by the executive branch of government (a governor and his councillors).

Perhaps that was why the rate set for composition and printing of the *Statutes* was somewhat higher than average. This, the Queen's Printer justified on the grounds of the legal requirement for absolute accuracy. According to the Queen's Printer's rivals, the *Canada Gazette* was also a profitable publication since it was filled entirely with paid advertising submitted by government and the other organizations that were required to insert notices. Both publications were given large press runs and were lavishly distributed. In addition, the Queen's Printer was still free to publish as many extra copies as he could sell to the general public.

However, the printing Desbarats and Derbishire did under their letters patent accounted for only a small fraction of the requirements of the legislative and executive branches of government. Besides the printing of the *Statutes* and the *Canada Gazette*,

the government gave a substantial amount of other work to the Queen's Printer and, at the same time, patronized other printers who had no official status. The executive branches of government were gradually evolving into departments. As their output of reports and other documents grew, so did their demand for printing, which was ordered either from the Queen's Printer, or from outside firms, and paid for on the basis of a schedule of fixed prices.

In the legislature, the two Houses each appointed a committee to look after the printing of the sessional records such as the journals, committee and special reports, and other returns tabled in Parliament. Each session, the two committees either appointed their own suppliers, or awarded contracts on the basis of competitive tenders. Separate contracts for printing, binding and for the supply of printing paper were usually awarded to the lowest bidders in each category. The committees also decided how many copies of each publication were to be printed. Some were issued in limited numbers for members of the House, while extra copies, often in large quantities, were ordered for general distribution.

Under these separate systems, executive and legislative expenditures for printing, binding and stationery increased dramatically year by year, until cost became a major problem. The legislature introduced various cost-cutting measures, all with limited success. There were probably several reasons why the suggested reforms often targeted the Queen's Printer's commission. This appointment had been made by a governor who was not responsible to the Legislative

Assembly, and was particularly annoying. Furthermore, the Queen's Printer's rates, also established independently by the governor (and suspected of being much too high), represented a large amount of political patronage which the Legislative Assembly wanted under its control. As early as 1844, the first of several bills was introduced to abolish the Queen's Printer's patent and open the monopoly to public competition. It was defeated, but various acts intended to reduce the cost of printing the *Statutes* were passed, and in 1850, Desbarats and Derbishire were forced to reduce the prices they charged government for advertising in the *Canada Gazette.*

Nevertheless, printing costs continued to mount. In 1851, the Committee on the Printing of the Legislative Assembly began a series of inquiries to determine why printing cost so much. The Committee was particularly suspicious of the Queen's Printer, and rival printers naturally did little to discourage that view. All who testified thought that most of the printing under the commission should be awarded on the basis of competitive tenders. John Lovell, an important printer often employed by the legislature, suggested the only way to obtain cheaper rates would be to contract all the printing for Parliament and for the government departments from one printer for a period of several years. This would allow the successful contractor sufficient time to recover the outlay for the necessary equipment. Another printer, Hugh Scobie, disagreed. He said that giving so much work to one contractor would simply create another monopoly, since few printing offices were large

enough to compete for the work. In any case, a contract system would only work, he warned, "provided the system pursued by the heads of departments is to be abandoned of bestowing the work upon political partizans." [*sic*] Derbishire countered with price lists to show that in some cases the Queen's Printer's rates were actually lower than what was being paid to parliamentary printing contractors. He said that if he and Desbarats were given all the printing done for the legislature and the government departments, they would reduce their prices by 30 percent.

Members of the Committee on Printing charged that "their efforts to obtain full and explicit information have been frustrated by delays or evaded by indistinct and unsatisfactory answers to enquiries which would have elucidated much of the mystery which had involved this question." However, they were able to recommend the following:

On the one hand, a judicious curtailment of all documents referred to the Printing Press, so as to avoid surplusage without impairing utility; and on the other, the adoption of means to obtain reduced prices, whereby the double economy of making your printing less in amount, and lower in cost may be insured; would seem to be obvious remedial suggestions suited to the case.

Subsequently the two committees on printing of the legislature adopted a policy of reviewing all reports tabled in both Houses before ordering them to

A Contractor Responds to Reform

In 1859, when Parliament established the Joint Committee on Printing, the parliamentary printing contract was held by Samuel Thompson. Trained as a practical printer, Thompson was also a newspaper editor, a publisher, and an author. In his autobiography, *Reminiscences of a Canadian Pioneer for the Last Fifty Years*, published in 1884, he described the often difficult life of a government contractor.

Thompson believed that his practical experience as a printer gave him an advantage over most other contractors, and in 1858, allowed him to secure the parliamentary printing contract with a bid slightly lower than the one tendered by the former supplier. He closed his Toronto newspaper business, followed the legislature to Quebec, and set up another printing plant for the government work. There he also began to publish an inexpensive newspaper, and in 1860, released *Thompson's Mirror of Parliament*, a forerunner of the official *Hansard*.

By Thompson's account, his defeated rival, who bore him a "violent grudge," had in the meantime joined forces with a former contractor for French-language printing, and with the Queen's Printer, "to destroy my credit, to entice away my workmen, to disseminate but too successfully the falsehood, that my contract was taken at unprofitable rates." But despite such stiff opposition, Thompson remained confident of success. Indeed, it was not so much the work of his opponents, but rather the ac-

tion of the legislature itself, that eventually forced him into bankruptcy.

Thompson could not have anticipated how his many business ventures would be affected by the reforms of parliamentary printing introduced in 1859. As the Joint Committee on Printing reduced the amount

Samuel Thompson

of printing to be ordered, it also eliminated much of the work which Thompson had been prepared to do. "Thus were one-half of all my expenditures — one-half of my thirty thousand dollars worth of type — one-half of my fifteen thousand dollars worth of presses and machinery — literally rendered useless, and reduced to the condi-

tion of second-hand material."

Faced with this setback, Thompson struggled on until his creditors, who were influenced by the rumour that his contract rates were unrealistically low, abandoned him. The firm went under, but Thompson still refused to give up.

Among his faithful employees were four young men of means who, Thompson said, were also excellent printers. At the bailiff's sale, these four acquired enough of the print shop to carry on the contract work, and in less than a month, the office was set up again, and the parliamentary printing well in hand. Thompson was back in business, with four new partners.

But the respite was short-lived. Thompson was accused by some of the members, including Cartier, of having slandered French Canadian institutions in his newspaper. During the ensuing imbroglio, the print shop was threatened with arson. Rather than expose his partners to complete ruin, Thompson decided to sell his share of the business, and return to Toronto.

For Samuel Thompson, the reforms in government printing led to personal catastrophe. But his partners continued to carry out the parliamentary printing at the established contract rates, thus vindicating their mentor's claim that his prices were fair and reasonable. Two of the partners, Robert Hunter and George Maclean Rose, formed Hunter, Rose and Company, an important Canadian publishing house, and continued as printers to Parliament for nearly a decade.

be printed. As a result, fewer reports were printed, and some were printed in abstract only. The *Journals* and other parliamentary publications were printed on smaller pages in a reduced type size. Another recommendation that all government printing be obtained under one contract was not implemented.

Despite these efforts to reduce costs, printing, binding, stationery and related services continued to become more expensive each year. In 1858, the Committee on the Printing of the Legislative Assembly estimated that these costs had reached at least $350,000: "a sum alike out of all proportion to the public revenue, as well as to the actual exigencies of the public service."

More drastic steps were required to reduce printing costs. In 1859, the Joint Committee on Printing was established to represent both Houses of the legislature. This committee initiated yet another major inquiry into the cost of printing and declared:

. . . if the Government, at an early day, had attached a Printing Office and Bindery to the Legislative Departments, many of the evils and extravagances which have grown upon the country, and a very large proportion of the money cost would have been saved.

In 1859, such a step was not even considered as a realistic alternative. However, the Joint Committee was at least able to reform the procedures affecting the printing performed for the two Houses of Parliament. Under its new centralized system of control, much duplicate and unnecessary printing was eliminated.

Many printers had testified that they could print more cheaply if they were guaranteed more work over a longer period of time, so the Joint Committee on Printing recommended that all the printing for both Houses be given to one printing contractor, for a specified number of years. Consequently, five-year contracts were awarded on the basis of tenders, with the result that, during the Joint Committee's first year, parliamentary printing costs were reduced by about 50 percent, and in 1860, by an additional 75 percent, that is, from $110,000 to $26,000.

The Committee was also concerned that the work performed by the Queen's Printer should be done more cheaply under competitive tenders; that fewer documents should be printed; and that fewer copies should be distributed. But, though Parliament's printing arrangements had been thoroughly overhauled, for the time being, the Queen's Printer's commission remained unaffected by these reforms.

In 1862, the Auditor General more or less confirmed charges that "much of the government printing was distributed by means an outsider could only guess at." He reported that the departmental printing and stationery accounts, which were impossible to audit, constituted the largest single item under the government's contingencies budget.

If the Queen's Printer had enjoyed a lucrative business in 1841, 20 years later—partly because of the growth of the departments—the office's profits had grown to astonishing proportions. George Edward Desbarats, son of the Queen's Printer, estimated that the family's printing plants produced, without tenders, approximately one-third of all the departmental printing, over and above that done under the Queen's Printer's commission. Payment for this came to approximately $100,000 per year. It is impossible to know exactly how much profit was included in this sum; but undoubtedly it was generous.

It is hardly surprising that demands to abolish the Queen's Printer's commission were becoming too frequent to ignore. Some members of the Legislative Assembly wanted the *Canada Gazette* and the *Statutes*, as well as departmental printing, placed under the same type of competitive contracts as parliamentary printing. The public was also ready for a change. Like James Young (Member for Waterloo), they regarded the Queen's Printership as, "the most expensive luxury about the Capital, and thought

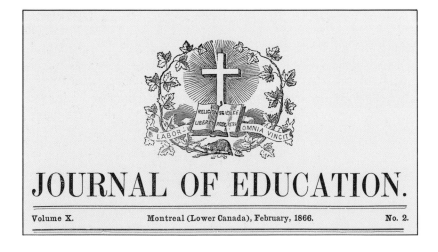

that it was quite time to introduce principles of retrenchment."

The government might have done so in April 1863, when Stewart Derbishire died, whereby the jointly held patent became void. However, according to John A. Macdonald, the Reform Ministry was afraid that Malcolm Cameron (Member for St. Clair) "was about to make some inconvenient motion in the Upper House,—a motion that would, doubtless, have proved disagreeable to the Government then existing." Rather than face such a motion from the unpredictable Cameron, the government renewed the Queen's Printer's commission in the face of overwhelming opposition. The consequences proved profitable to Cameron, who had had little to do with printing. By letters made patent on April 20, 1863, he succeeded Derbishire, and joined George-Paschal Desbarats as Queen's Printer. In 1864, when a deputy minister at the helm of a government department might have earned $3,200 annually, Desbarats arranged to pay his new partner $12,000, a sum which represented Cameron's share of profits earned for printing the *Canada Gazette* and the *Statutes*. The partnership turned out to be a brief one, since George-Paschal Desbarats died the following year.

This time the government seized "the opportunity offered by the lamented death of George Desbarats, Esquire," on November 12, 1864, by recommending, two days later, that the Queen's Printer's office be reorganized. The Provincial Secretary was asked to review and report upon the subject immediately. However, during the Confederation years, Parliament

Malcolm Cameron

The last Canadian Queen's Printer ever appointed under a commission to the Crown, was an important political reformer described by contemporaries as "at times too outspoken, both for his own good—measured in the light of selfish considerations—and the cause to be favoured." Malcolm Cameron's uncompromising principles and impetuous nature often turned him from a zealous ally into an equally zealous opponent, "utterly indifferent as to who felt the shafts of his wit and railery, so long as he succeeded in accomplishing an object in view." During a long and erratic political career, Cameron attacked as often as supported Reform Party ministries.

Cameron, the son of Presbyterian Scots, was born in 1808, in Trois-Rivières, but spent much of his childhood near Perth, in Upper Canada. Like his American contemporary, Abraham Lincoln, whom he greatly admired, Cameron was an idealist, and a self-made man. As a teenager, he is said to have rebelled against a tyrannical employer by walking, in defiance of the harsh winter weather, from La Prairie, Lower Canada, to Montreal—"I preferred frost to slavery"—where he found another job, as a stable boy. The youth had little opportunity to attend school, but read widely to expand his knowledge before going into business by opening a general store.

In 1833 Cameron visited Scotland and brought back a wife, his cousin Christina McGregor. Soon his business interests expanded. He dealt heavily in real estate near Perth and at Port Sarnia, where he also invested in flour and lumber mills, and in shipbuilding. In 1837, to allow himself more time for personal supervision over his many commercial projects, Cameron moved to the

Malcolm Cameron
Her Majesty's Printer and Law Printer 1863–1869

"I am a radical of radicals and have no sympathy with those who want to stand still."

Cameron was appointed Queen's Printer jointly with George-Paschal Desbarats. After Desbarats' death in 1864, Cameron's imprint continued to appear on the *Canada Gazette* until the Queen's Printer's Act came into force October 1, 1869.

area and became a founder of the town of Sarnia.

There he established a weekly newspaper, *The Bathurst Courier*, which he was forced to sell a year later because the wealthy and Tory merchants refused to advertise in an independent paper that proclaimed to be the "slave or tool" of no party. In 1836, Cameron was elected as a moderate Reformer in Lanark County to the Upper Canada Assembly. But when a bill (which he supported) for selling the clergy reserve land was rushed through on the last night of a session, Cameron, who was a temperance advocate, was outraged that this had been accomplished through force and drunkenness. He declared himself independent and swore never to enter the House again. After missing one session, he ran again and sat in the first Assembly of the United Province of Canada. Until his appointment as Queen's Printer, Cameron successfully contested every election but one, and held a variety of important portfolios.

By 1850, Cameron began to act with a new radical movement, which became known by a name supposedly coined from one of his own pithy exclamations: "They call us gritty—yes we are, and Clear Grit at that."

As a member of the Legislative Assembly, and later as a member of the Legislative Council, Cameron fought for temperance, and for progressive causes such as the defeat of the Family Compact and the establishment of responsible government, the separation of church and state, confederation, the right of women to own property, and the abolition of imprisonment for debt.

In 1862, he visited British Columbia, became quite popular and was appointed by the people to go to England where he secured self-government for their colony. One year later, Cameron's appointment as Queen's Printer with George-Paschal Desbarats ended all this excitement. Cameron likely accepted the position because his finances had become "irretrievably embarrassed." But despite a handsome income from this commission, his financial prospects never improved.

After his term as Queen's Printer expired, Cameron repeatedly tried to re-enter politics. Finally, in 1874, he was elected to the House of Commons as a Liberal for South Ontario. He died while still a member on June 1, 1876.

Cameron acquired the name, "the coon," (a reference to his raccoon coat), during an election which he lost, despite having taunted his opponent with insults and threats of a "coon hunt on the Wabash." This cartoon, which appeared in *Canadian Illustrated News* on April 1, 1876, satirized the notion that either political party was "above the other as regards purity and immunity from corruption." Cameron is depicted with a list of election expenses, as "the coon up the tree." Topping the list is the cost of printing *The Ottawa Times*, a partisan newspaper, the owners of which had obtained lucrative government printing contracts.

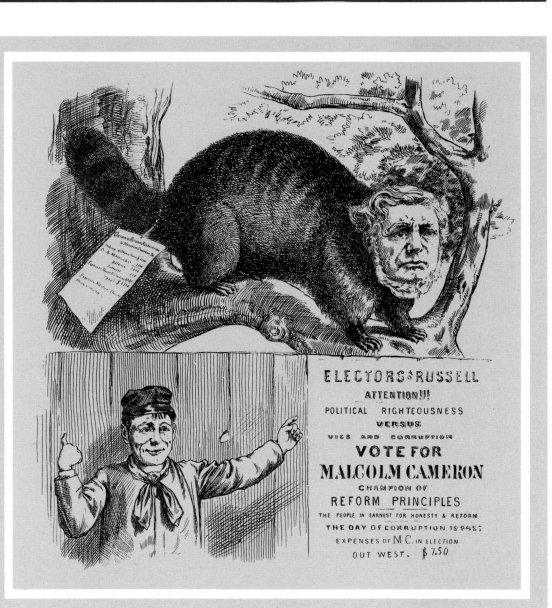

was concerned with many pressing matters besides the reorganization of government printing, and nothing was done about the Queen's Printer for some time. Whenever complaints about printing were heard in the legislature, Prime Minister Macdonald responded that the matter was still "under consideration."

Meanwhile, George-Paschal Desbarats' son, George Edward, continued a thriving printing business. Although Malcolm Cameron's imprint continued provisionally to appear on the *Canada Gazette* and the *Statutes*, it was George Edward who printed and distributed them. Desbarats also had a lucrative contract for the supply of parliamentary printing paper; he was confidential printer to the government; and in 1865, after a Quebec contractor's bindery was destroyed by fire, he did the binding for Parliament as well. Since it was business as usual in Desbarats' establishment, it is hardly surprising that contemporaries sometimes mistakenly referred to George Edward as "Queen's Printer." Not until October 1, 1869, did the government finally make other arrangements for its printing.

*When the Government shall be settled per-
manently in one place, and the expenses of
frequent removals, losses by the accidents of
travel . . . and the necessary erection of costly
buildings, adapted to an extensive printing business, shall cease to be part of the ordinary outlay
of the Queen's Printer, a plan of retrenchment
may no doubt be devised and submitted to
the Government.*

Derbishire and Desbarats,
responding to the Joint Committee on Printing,
when asked to suggest "any plan" that
might reduce costs, 1859

espite all the criticism that the office of Queen's Printer received during the period of the Union Government, between 1841 and 1867, it was often said, with particular reference to George-Paschal Desbarats, that "perhaps no printing office in the world was better managed than that of the Province under his management."

To serve the needs of the Union Government, Desbarats and Derbishire had

The government of the Province of Canada, and the establishment of its official printer, became peripatetic after an angry mob destroyed the Parliament buildings in Montreal in 1849. During the fire, Stewart Derbishire, a book lover, was seen rushing about the building, his arms piled high with tomes from the Parliamentary Library.

to establish not just one, but several printing plants in Kingston, Montreal, Toronto, Quebec and finally Ottawa—all cities which hosted sessions of Parliament at one time or another. This often required the transfer of printing supplies and equipment from city to city. Though we know little about these establishments, evidence submitted by the Queen's Printer at different times to the Joint Committee on Printing does provide some information about how the official print shops were run.

Desbarats and Derbishire's patent required them to maintain a large plant and numerous staff, since both the *Canada Gazette* and the *Statutes* involved much printing at a moment's notice. After receiving royal assent at the end of each session, the bound volumes of the *Statutes* had to be ready for distribution as soon as possible. Consequently, the printing of what was in those days a large number of impressions had to proceed with the greatest possible speed.

As Desbarats and Derbishire were not appointed Queen's Printer until September 29, 1841, fully 11 days after the close of the provincial Parliament's first session in Kingston, they had to set up for their new duties in great haste. Nonetheless, Derbishire reported that they managed to issue a complete edition of that session's *Statutes* in just seven weeks. This was less time than had been customary under the old administrations of Upper and Lower Canada. Still, Desbarats and Derbishire felt there was much room for improvement, and without being told to do so, determined to convert to steam-powered presses for printing the *Statutes*.

During those years, the use of steam power to operate printing presses was quite new, at least in British North America. Desbarats and Derbishire were perhaps unaware that William Cunnabell of Halifax had been the first to run a printing press under steam power a year earlier, in 1840. Nonetheless, they were eager to experiment with the new technology. By the time Parliament's second session ended on October 12, 1842, the Queen's Printer's establishment was ready with two steam-powered presses. On these presses the entire edition of 6,000 copies of the *Statutes* was turned out in three weeks, less than half the time required a year earlier. Again in 1843, 6,000 copies of a large edition of the *Statutes*, comprising 420 pages, were ready for distribution in just over one month. These results are particularly impressive because the type from bills printed for consideration by Parliament was not kept standing for the subsequent printing of the bills in their final form, as acts of Parliament. Before the acts that had received royal assent could be promulgated, the printers had to set the type, print the sheets and bind them into volumes for distribution.

In 1844, when the seat of government was moved from Kingston to Montreal, the Queen's Printer erected a five-storey building on Ste. Thérèse Street, at the corner of St. Gabriel, to serve as the government printing office. Robert Romaine, the Superintendent, was in charge of the installation of the plant and machinery, which he described as including "machine presses" and a steam engine. Many years later, Romaine claimed that this work

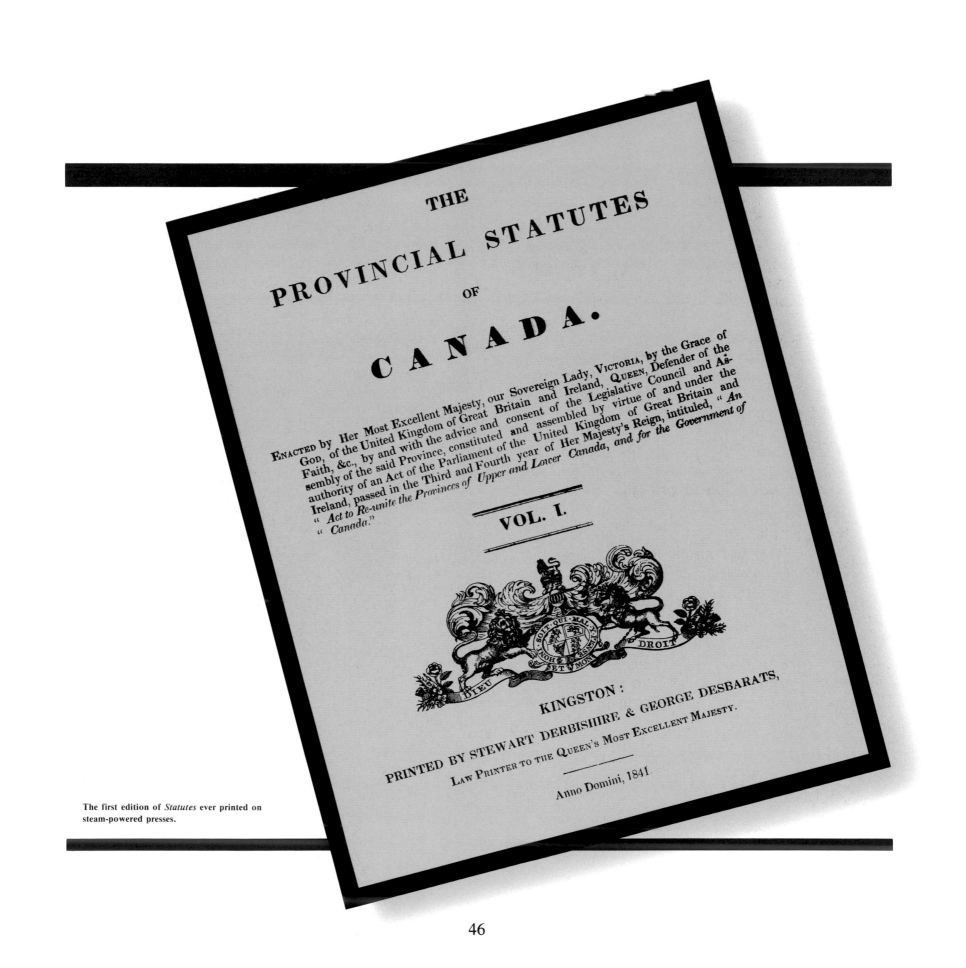

THE

PROVINCIAL STATUTES

OF

CANADA.

Enacted by Her Most Excellent Majesty, our Sovereign Lady, Victoria, by the Grace of God, of the United Kingdom of Great Britain and Ireland, Queen, Defender of the Faith, &c., by and with the advice and consent of the Legislative Council and Assembly of the said Province, constituted and assembled by virtue of and under the authority of an Act of the Parliament of the United Kingdom of Great Britain and Ireland, passed in the Third and Fourth year of Her Majesty's Reign, intituled, "An Act to Re-unite the Provinces of Upper and Lower Canada, and for the Government of Canada."

VOL. I.

KINGSTON :

PRINTED BY STEWART DERBISHIRE & GEORGE DESBARATS,

Law Printer to the Queen's Most Excellent Majesty.

Anno Domini, 1841.

The first edition of *Statutes* ever printed on steam-powered presses.

made him "the first printer in Canada to introduce steam printing in 1844." However, in making this claim, he seemed to have forgotten, or been unaware of, the earlier use of steam power in the Queen's Printer's establishment in Kingston.

Though the Queen's Printer's Montreal establishment was not the first, it was certainly among the earliest offices in Canada to use steam-powered cylinder presses. John Lovell's print shop in Montreal did not have a steam press until 1847; and the *Montreal Gazette* did not convert to steam power until 1853, the year it was purchased by John Lowe and Brown Chamberlin, a future Queen's Printer. Before that, the paper's cylinder press was powered by two men working a flywheel.

Desbarats and Derbishire generally accepted the necessity of moving the printing facilities from city to city to follow the peripatetic legislature as an inevitable, if somewhat extravagant, part of their operation. However, in testimony before the Joint Committee on Printing, Derbishire tried to impress upon his clients just how cumbersome the continual roaming could be, by describing one occasion on which moving costs reached truly absurd proportions. In 1851, during the move from Toronto to Quebec, all the type, presses, stock and books from Desbarats and Derbishire's printing plant, as well as their private effects, were aboard the *Ottawa* when it sank in Lake Ontario.

A Business Statement from the Queen's Printer for 1850

The persons employed by the Queen's Printer are five Clerks and two Assistants, one Reader, one Foreman, one Assistant Foreman, one Keeper of Laws, one Engineer, six Pressmen, eight Boys, four Binders, six Folders, and from twenty-two to forty Compositors, varying from fifty-eight to seventy-six persons.

In order to supply the demands of the Government and of the public through it with greater dispatch, the Queen's Printer obtained Machine Presses, Machinery, Steam Engines wherewith to print with greater rapidity, and their stock of printing materials is as follows:—

A Steam Engine of five-horse power, pulleys, wheels, &c.
Two large cylinder Presses on most improved plans.
Four large hand Presses.
11,000 lbs. of Bourgeois type for "Gazette".
10,500 lbs. of Pica type for Laws.
3800 lbs. of small Pica for bills &c.
2,300 lbs. of Long Primer do.

1800 lbs. of Brevier for notes, &c.
500 lbs. of English for headings.
3,500 lbs. of types of various kinds for titles, jobs, &c., &c., for meeting the various orders from Government.
100 pairs of Chases, Cases, Racks, &c., &c., for the above types.
3 large standing Presses, Gas Fittings, water tanks, &c.
A large Bindery with all the materials and tools required, and a large assortment of stationery.

It has been settled that there shall be a salaried Officer to be styled "Queen's Printer", the salary to be $2,000 a year. He is to have the supervision of the publication of the Gazette & the Statutes, and such other work of a similar character, that may be ordered by the Government. . . . I do not suppose that you will consider the Office of "Queen's Printer" worth your acceptance. Should you, however, choose to accept it, I have authority to offer it to you.

Prime Minister John A. Macdonald,
writing to George Edward Desbarats,
May 14, 1869

uring the 1850s, Ottawa was an isolated, hard-drinking little lumber town. It seemed, at the time, an unlikely spot for the permanent seat of the legislature, but Queen Victoria chose it as a compromise over more prestigious cities such as Toronto, Montreal and Quebec. This was partly because Ottawa's position, directly on the border between the old provinces of Upper and Lower Canada, made it, according to the

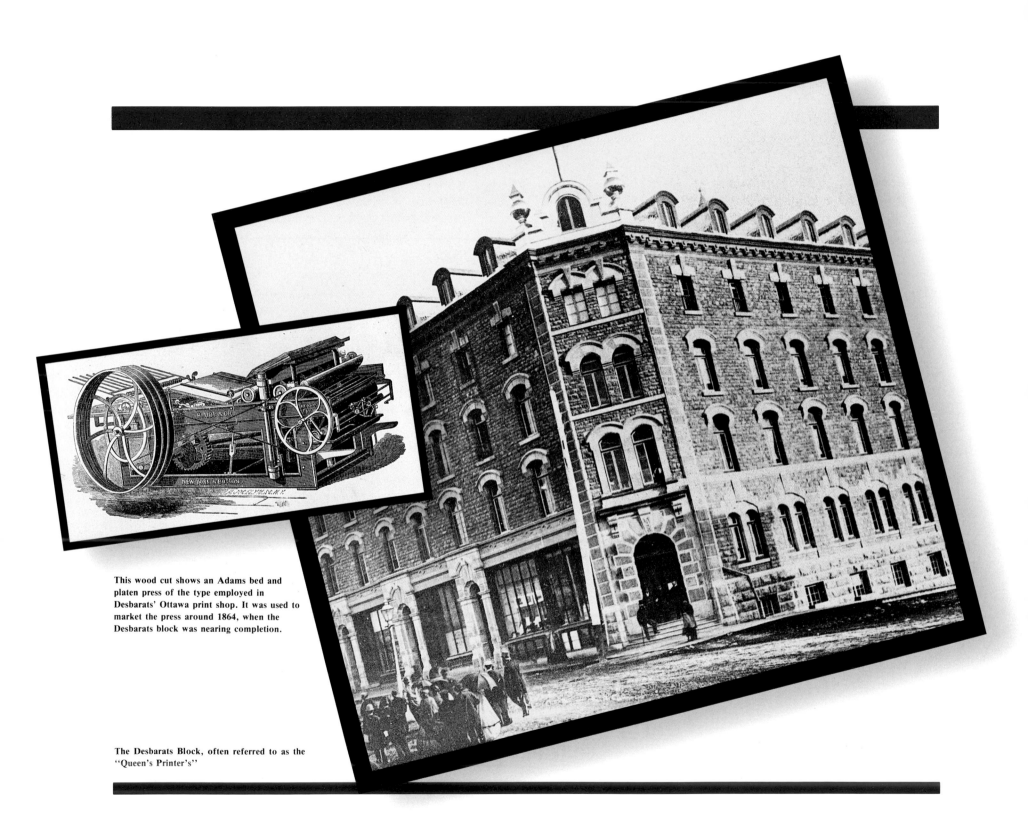

This wood cut shows an Adams bed and platen press of the type employed in Desbarats' Ottawa print shop. It was used to market the press around 1864, when the Desbarats block was nearing completion.

The Desbarats Block, often referred to as the "Queen's Printer's"

Governor General, Sir Edmund Head, the "least objectionable" place.

If Ottawa itself seemed at first unimpressive, at least its setting on the banks of the Ottawa River was spectacular, and its new status as the legislative capital quickly brought changes to the town. In 1867, George Edward Desbarats published a little Ottawa guide book in which he declared: "Its principal streets are of great width and extend from East to West nearly three miles, and throughout the whole of these, the meaner buildings are being gradually displaced by erections worthy of the large thoroughfares upon which they are situated."

The new Desbarats Block, or "Queen's Printer's," as it was also known, was (besides the parliamentary buildings themselves) probably the largest of these structures. Situated on the corner of Sparks and O'Connor streets, it was 132 feet long and four storeys high along Sparks; and 100 feet long and five storeys high along O'Connor. The massive structure not only housed a printing plant, but was also a sort of shopping centre with enough space for a bank, a railway office, a hat shop, a tailor and a boarding house run by a Mrs. Trotter. The upper storeys were used as private apartments; one of them was for Joseph Bureau, Desbarats' foreman.

The print shop itself, which *The Ottawa Citizen* was to call Canada's "finest and most elegantly fitted printing, stationery and bookbinding establishments," employed close to 100 people and occupied four storeys in the western end of the building. Large openings in the floors created a shaft through which material was hoisted up and down between the four levels. Because of the weight of the printing presses, the pressroom was in the basement. It boasted six steam-powered presses: three Hoe cylinder presses, one of them very large, for newspapers and periodicals such as the *Canada Gazette*, and three Adams bed and platen presses for fine book work. There was also a lathe for repairs and an addressing machine for distribution. The steam engine and boiler were in an adjacent room. Long belts connected to the engine ran throughout the building to power the presses, bindery equipment and the hoisting apparatus.

At street level, Desbarats' retail shop supplied the public with stationery and "fancy goods." The clerical offices and storerooms were also on the ground floor. One flight up, the composing room carried an immense quantity of type; "probably the largest amount of material in the Dominion," thought a reporter from *The Ottawa Citizen*. The bindery, on the third floor, enjoyed an excellent reputation. The same reporter continued, "The work turned out here, by 20 to 30 hands, was of a very fine quality, some specimens of which took a gold medal at the Paris Exposition, and others received honourable mention."

But even with the growth that typified Ottawa's early years as the capital, the city had its share of uneasiness. Much of this was caused by the Fenian Brotherhood, a revolutionary society of Irish Americans. For years they had been threatening to invade and conquer Canada, in order to use the country as a base of operations for the liberation of Ireland from Britain. After the end of the American

Civil War, with their ranks boosted by discharged war veterans and by Irish immigrants to the United States, the Fenians seemed especially menacing. A Fenian government for Canada was actually established in New York City, where men were enlisted in an Irish Republican Army. Generals were appointed, and arsenals were established for the collection of arms intended for the capture of Canada.

Early in 1866, with reports of a massive Fenian invasion planned for St. Patrick's Day, Canada's militia sprang to arms. Almost overnight, some 10,000 volunteers were called out and stationed along the frontier. The crisis continued for months, with reports of hundreds of Fenians massing at various points in the United States along the Canadian border. In June, as Parliament was about to meet for the first session

to be held in the new capital, organized forces of Fenians crossed into Canadian territory on the Quebec and Niagara frontiers. The Canadians drove them back with difficulty, and with loss of life on both sides.

While these invasions caused some disruptions at the Queen's Printer's (the staff joined the Civil Service Rifle Regiment), the Fenians were responsible for another shocking event that involved the establishment much more directly. On the night of April 6, 1868, as the Irish-Canadian member of Parliament, Thomas D'Arcy McGee, was returning home to Mrs. Trotter's boarding house in the Desbarats Block, he was assassinated at the door in front of the building. A Fenian extremist was convicted of the crime.

The Civil Service Up in Arms

During the Fenian crisis of 1866, Ottawa's civil servants, who could not be spared from their official duties, were organized into the Civil Service Rifle Regiment. Service was mandatory for all male civil servants aged 18 to 45. It was understood that this regiment would not be called for service away from the capital, but to these men was entrusted "the guard and care of the Public Buildings and the Archives, whilst they will at the same time be enabled to continue their several official duties." The Queen's Printer offered his men (who were not actually civil servants) to form a portion of the regiment, an offer which John A. Macdonald accepted:

... it is of importance, that in all cases the Queen's Printer should have his full complement of men, to perform the duties of his office, and it would be extremely inconvenient that they should be drawn away from the Seat of Government on service.

Bolstered by nearly 100 of Desbarats' employees, the Civil Service Rifle Regiment numbered 338 officers and men. Ottawa became in some ways an armed camp, and George Edward Desbarats became a commissioned officer.

Of course, the Fenians never got as far as Ottawa, so the Civil Service Rifle Regiment saw no action, but had plenty of time for marching, drills and other such excitements. The Desbarats family still owns a silver tray decorated with the regiment's crest and inscribed: "Officers Match—first prize won by Captain Desbarats October 1867."

Pressroom squad of the Civil Service Rifle Regiment in 1867

George Edward Desbarats placed a commemorative plaque on the wall of his building to mark the spot where McGee had been murdered. For this, he received several threatening letters from the Fenians, but apparently did not take them seriously.

Nine months later, on the night of January 20, 1869, a magnificent costume ball, which George Edward had arranged as a surprise for his wife, Lucianne, was held at Desbarats' home on Chapel Street. It was one of the most sensational social events so far held at the new capital. "Everybody came, and everyone had taken pains with their costumes," Lucianne noted in her diary. And then she described how, just as she was leading the guests to supper, a man from the printing plant rushed in shouting, "Your building is on fire!"

When they received the news, Georges, Charles and Morrin tore off their costumes and rushed away. Left alone with all the guests, the centre of attention, I was in an awkward position. I gave the signal to the band to play God Save the Queen. Then everyone left.

The sheriff, a rifle brigade, all the town's fire engines and nearly all its citizens turned out for the conflagration. Arrayed as Richelieus, clowns, heroes and kings, the guests from the costume ball also rushed to the burning building and tried to save it. But the fire was fuelled by tremendous amounts of paper stock and drafted by the openings in the floors,

and Ottawa had no running water. Within two hours, the entire building was reduced to smouldering ruins. The Desbarats family was convinced that Fenians were responsible for the catastrophe, and had chosen that night as a spectacular occasion to take their revenge and burn down the Queen's Printer's establishment.

Besides the building, George Edward had lost his new equipment, type and $100,000 worth of stock. Suddenly without a print shop, under what must have been desperate circumstances, he made hasty arrangements to carry on. The very next day, *The Ottawa Times* reported:

Yesterday morning Mr. Desbarats commenced arrangements for continuing his business, in which, we understand, he was freely assisted by the other establishments in the city, so that as little public inconvenience as possible, under the circumstances, may be expected to result from the calamity.

Four months later, in May 1869, Prime Minister Macdonald was able to advise George Edward Desbarats that the government had at last come to a decision about the Queen's Printer. There was still to be a Queen's Printer, but in future, the title holder would be an officer of the government. The profits formerly accruing to the Queen's Printer under the patent for printing, distribution and sale of the *Canada Gazette* and the *Statutes* were to be taken away. Instead, the printing and binding were to be opened to public competition and executed by private

The charred ruins of Desbarats' building after it was destroyed in a spectacular fire on January 20, 1869. There was speculation that the fire was the work of Fenian sympathizers, who were angered by the commemorative plaque which George Edward had attached to his building.

HERE FELL
ON THE
7th April 1868.
BY THE
ASSASSIN'S HAND
THOMAS D'ARCY
McGEE

PLEASE DO NOT TOUCH

54

George Edward Desbarats
The Dominion's First Queen's Printer

Although George-Paschal Desbarats' son, George Edward, eventually became a great Canadian publisher, it took him some time to settle on that career. Born in Quebec on April 5, 1838, he attended Jesuit schools in Massachusetts and in Montreal. He was admitted to the bar in 1859 and worked as a lawyer for a year or two before he became active in his father's printing business.

Besides running the government printing office in Quebec, the two Desbarats, father and son, produced many important literary, cultural, historical and religious book titles. Before leaving Quebec to follow the government to Ottawa, George Edward met the literary elite of Quebec society, some of whom would later contribute to his many publications. Notable among them was Father Charles Honoré Laverdière, editor of the six-volume *Oeuvres de Champlain*, George Edward's most ambitious book publishing venture.

After resigning his position as Queen's Printer in 1870, George Edward Desbarats went on to launch a wide variety of new journals in quick succession. Among them were *The Canadian Patent Office Record and Mechanic's Magazine* and *Canada Medical and Surgical Journal*. In 1872, he commenced publication of *The Favourite*, a magazine devoted to serialized fiction.

At the same time, Desbarats was busy developing new commercial applications for the inventions of his business partner, William Augustus Leggo. The most daring,

George Edward Desbarats, Queen's Printer 1869-1870.

and possibly the most costly scheme, was the formation of a company with investors in Montreal and New York, to launch the world's first illustrated daily newspaper, *The Daily Graphic*, published in New York between 1873 and 1889. According to George Edward's great-grandson, Peter Desbarats, the paper is generally recognized as being the world's first illustrated daily newspaper, and also as the first daily to print experimental half-tone photographs.

By 1874, the Desbarats fortune could no longer keep pace with the scope of George Edward's vision, and he was forced to declare personal bankruptcy. He was 36 years old.

But Desbarats was not easily defeated. Two years later, he started over again by opening a small printing office in Montreal. In 1877, his 15-year-old son, William, joined him, and soon their company began once more to prosper. In 1887, they launched a splendid new magazine full of glossy half-tone photographs. *The Dominion Illustrated*, established nearly 20 years after the *Canadian Illustrated News*, at a time when half-tone photographic reproduction had finally become a more established art, was still one of the first magazines in Canada to fully exploit the process. This magazine outlived George Edward. He died in 1893 at the age of 54.

William, his son, built the Desbarats Printing Company into one of Canada's largest commercial printing houses, an establishment which remained in the family until 1969.

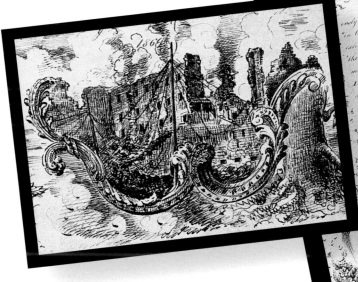

The citizens of Ottawa presented George Edward Desbarats with this handsome testimonial. It expresses sympathy for Desbarats, whose building had been destroyed by fire, and the hope that he would, nevertheless, remain in the city.

firms under five-year contracts, which were to be supervised by the Queen's Printer.

It has been settled that there shall be a salaried Officer to be styled "Queen's Printer", the salary to be $2,000 a year. He is to have the supervision of the publication of the Gazette & the Statutes, and such other work of a similar character, that may be ordered by the Government. . . . I do not suppose that you will consider the Office of "Queen's Printer" worth your acceptance. Should you, however, choose to accept it, I have the authority to offer it to you.

Printing for the government departments was also to be done under contract and to become the Queen's Printer's responsibility. Thus the Queen's Printer, as a civil servant, would in effect supervise a series of contracts in much the same way that the Joint Committee on the Printing of Parliament supervised its own separate printing contracts.

"An Act respecting the Office of Queen's Printer and the Public Printing" received royal assent on June 22, and came into force October 1, 1869. On that day, two years after Confederation, George Edward Desbarats became a civil servant.

Becoming Canada's first Queen's Printer at the age of 31 was in itself an impressive achievement, but for the relatively young Desbarats (who often used the English translation of the name, Georges-Édouard), the appointment was just one of his many remarkable accomplishments as a printer and publisher. George Edward had a passion for all kinds of inventions. As a publisher, he was fascinated by illustrated journalism —particularly by the efforts of his peers to bring photography, still a relatively recent invention, to the printed page. This fascination had begun to absorb most of Desbarats' time, energy and capital by 1869, when Prime Minister Macdonald offered him the opportunity to become the new Dominion's first Queen's Printer.

Inasmuch as Desbarats was already deeply involved in a new partnership with an engraver, William Augustus Leggo, in Montreal and was well on the way to launching the most important publishing ventures of his career, it is surprising that he decided to accept a civil service job paying only $2,000 a year. Perhaps a sense of family tradition led him to accept the position of Queen's Printer. After all, the title would make George Edward the third Desbarats to serve as an official government printer in British North America. Then again, his wife Lucianne's practical influence may have entered into the decision:

He accepted the offer of the government with a great deal of reluctance but I myself think that 500 louis is worth more than I don't know how much in Leggotype, in which he has invested foolish amounts. If that fails, there will at least be 500 louis guaranteed.

"Leggotype" was a new photo-engraving process that William Augustus Leggo had patented in 1865. In Montreal, in October 1869, during the month in

In printing this photograph, George Edward Desbarats and his engraver, William Augustus Leggo, were ahead of anyone else in the world. In 1869, other magazines were still limited to illustrations produced by the artist's hand, engravings that resulted in black lines on white paper. But Leggo's half-tone produced a truly photographic image on the page. Like half-tones produced today, it is made up of a grid of hundreds of tiny dots that the human eye perceives as a pattern of light and shadow. Though experimental half-tone screens were at that time being tested, the process did not employ a printing surface in relief, and was therefore unsuitable for the letterpress printing of newspapers or magazines. Leggo's Granulated Photography process enabled him to make a photographic image on a durable printing plate, that would stand up to long print runs on steam-powered presses. For the first time, anything that could be photographed, theoretically could be printed in a widely circulated publication.

which he became Queen's Printer, George Edward Desbarats and his partner launched the first really successful Canadian illustrated news magazine. On the cover of the first issue of the *Canadian Illustrated News* appeared a half-tone reproduction of a photograph of Prince Arthur, taken by Montreal photographer William Notman. The half-tone was produced through a refinement of Leggo's photo-engraving process which he called "Granulated Photography."

Launching an illustrated news magazine was in itself a gamble in Canada because the country's relatively small population centres were isolated by vast distances. Publishing a Canadian magazine to test photo-engraving techniques was a truly astonishing undertaking.

No sooner was the *Canadian Illustrated News* launched than Desbarats inaugurated a French-language weekly newsmagazine, *L'Opinion publique*, in January 1870. *L'Opinion publique* contained original literary material and editorials, but its foreign reports were taken mainly from French publications.

Desbarats, who must have been commuting between Ottawa and Montreal at a frantic pace, was eventually forced to acknowledge the growing conflict between his two careers. In April 1870, after only a few months as Queen's Printer, he gave up the position and devoted himself entirely to his growing commitments in Montreal. Within two months, on June 7, Prime Minister Macdonald appointed Brown Chamberlin, a popular Conservative member of Parliament from the Eastern Townships, to be the second Queen's Printer for Canada.

A former editor of the *Montreal Gazette*, Chamberlin was on intimate terms with many influential Conservative politicians and enjoyed a

William Augustus Leggo Desbarats' Partner

For Desbarats, with his penchant for innovation and his family tradition of generations of master printers in Europe and North America, the engraver/inventor William Augustus Leggo was in many ways a perfect partner. Leggo had emigrated from Germany to Canada with his three brothers, all engravers. Their father had been trained in the lithographic process by Aloys Senefelder, the inventor of lithography.

Leggo invented a cheap and reliable way to print line images by transferring them photographically to a plate, which was then etched to obtain a relief printing surface suitable for ordinary letterpresses. This process was referred to as Leggotype. Desbarats claimed that he was able to sell an 1867 guidebook to Ottawa at a low price because the line drawings of parliamentary and departmental buildings had been obtained by this process.

Leggotype's first important application came after the disastrous 1869 fire at the Desbarats Block. Among the ruins of the building were all the type and the sheets for the *Oeuvres de Champlain*. Fortunately, before the fire, a set of galley proofs had been sent to the editor, Father Laverdière, in Quebec. Based on these proofs, Desbarats was able to publish a Leggotype edition of the book in 1870.

William Augustus Leggo

considerable following. After Confederation in 1867, John A. Macdonald had exhorted him to "work like a Trojan to return our friends [to Parliament] and all will be well." Chamberlin himself had won an easy victory at the polls in his riding of Missisquoi, handily defeating a former legislative councillor by more than two votes to one. That year, the new Montreal Printing and Publishing Company, established under

the direction of John Lowe, had acquired the property of *The Gazette* (formerly the *Montreal Gazette*), and Chamberlin began gradually to withdraw from his editorial responsibilities.

Never a wealthy man, Chamberlin was always obliged to live from his employment income. By his own account, it was thoughts of marriage and financial embarrassment that turned Chamberlin the

---

Brown Chamberlin
Longest Serving Queen's Printer

Brown Chamberlin, the son of Dr. Brown Chamberlin of Frelighsburg, Quebec, was born on March 26, 1827. After studying law at McGill University, Chamberlin was called to the bar in 1850, but he practised for only a short time before deciding that journalism would allow him more time to pursue his many other interests. Even during his student days, Chamberlin had demonstrated a literary bent. He worked as a frequent contributor to, and law reporter for, the *Montreal Gazette*. In 1852, he became editor and manager of the paper's literary department.

The following year, he bought the paper in partnership with his friend and brother-in-law, John Lowe, who later would be Deputy Minister of Agriculture. The two men were joint proprietors and editors until after Confederation, and under their editorial management the paper earned a high reputation.

The *Montreal Gazette* was one of the most influential Conservative newspapers, and Chamberlin wielded his editorial pen to further the interests of the Party. But he also examined many other subjects of special importance to him. One was the question of confederation, which he supported in editorial articles, speeches and essays, many of them published in leading British publications. According to an article that appeared shortly after Chamberlin's death, his early writings dismayed the future Fathers of Confederation, who were not yet ready to unite the country.

Another topic about which Chamberlin lectured and wrote extensively was Canadian industrial development. He attended the 1862 international exhibition in London as a Canadian exhibition commissioner.

A life-long Conservative, Chamberlin served Conservative governments for all but five years of his long career, and retired on November 7, 1891, just five months after the death of his mentor, Prime Minister John A. Macdonald. Brown Chamberlin died on July 13, 1897, at Lakefield, Ontario.

Brown Chamberlin, Queen's Printer 1870-1886,
Queen's Printer and Controller of Stationery 1886-1891.

In 1871, the Queen's Printer posed for this photograph with his wife, Agnes Chamberlin. Born Agnes Dunbar Moodie, she was the daughter of Susannah Moodie, and was herself a talented artist. She etched the lithographic stones and hand-coloured the plates for *Canadian Wild Flowers*, published in 1868. This book, said to be the first of its kind published in Canada, includes botanical descriptions by her aunt, Catherine Parr Traill.

politician into Chamberlin the office seeker. When George Edward Desbarats resigned, Chamberlin wrote to Prime Minister Macdonald asking for the Queen's Printership or some other appointment: "I have met with some misfortunes (pecuniarily) recently, but have had the great good fortune to find a woman who loves me dearly and would marry me. . . . You can make two people very happy at once."

At this point, fate intervened to make Chamberlin a popular choice for political appointment. On May 24, 1870, thousands of heavily armed Fenian troops began massing at many points along the Canada-United States border. Another invasion had been scheduled to coincide with Canadian celebrations of the Queen's birthday.

Chamberlin, who was a lieutenant-colonel in the

How the Queen's Printer Became a Hero

When the Fenians assembled on May 24, 1870, more than 13,000 Canadian volunteers and regulars were immediately called into active service and stationed at vulnerable points along the border. In Montreal, several thousand troops already assembled for Her Majesty's birthday parade had to be dispatched to the frontier.

Lieutenant-Colonel Chamberlin was far from the Eastern Townships and from the Sixtieth "Missisquoi" Battalion, of which he was to take immediate command. He had gone to Toronto, perhaps to celebrate the holiday with his fiancée. On his way to the front, Chamberlin stopped in Montreal just long enough to telegraph ahead to Frelighsburg. He instructed that local inhabitants with rifles should get together and try to hold Eccles Hill if it were not already occupied by Fenians.

Late that afternoon, Chamberlin managed to reach Stanbridge Station, a few miles from the contested Eccles Hill. Here, a handful of his battalion's 221 officers

The engagement at Eccles Hill. This illustration from the *Canadian Illustrated News* was based on a sketch prepared at the scene by George E. Desbarats' special correspondent. Thanks to the Leggotype process, subscribers were able to see it within a few days of the skirmish.

and men had assembled on short notice. Taking with him all the men he could muster, Chamberlin proceeded to the front. There he found that a group of about 35 farmers and local gentlemen calling themselves the "Dunham Boys" had managed to occupy Eccles Hill and had even captured two Fenian prisoners. Directly opposite the Canadian position, within a few hundred yards of the border, over 400 Fenians were already assembled. Clearly, on the Missisquoi frontier, Eccles Hill was to be the point of attack.

Chamberlin's commanding officer, Lieutenant-Colonel W. Osborne Smith of the militia, arrived the following morning. With five companies assembled in Montreal, Smith had marched overnight through heavy rains and deep mud, arriving at Stanbridge Station at daybreak. From there, Smith had ridden alone to Eccles Hill. Chamberlin, who had reinforced the 35 Dunham Boys with 38 officers and men from his battalion, had a combined force of only 73 men to resist an attack by over 400 Fenians. However, the Canadians were in well-protected positions and, from his hilltop lookout, Lieutenant-Colonel Chamberlin had a clear view of the entire frontier. Meanwhile, since the Fenians were sending for more reinforcements, Lieutenant-Colonel Smith rushed back to Stanbridge to bring up the remainder of the force, leaving Chamberlin in command.

But the attack came much sooner than anticipated, long before Smith could return with the reserves from Stanbridge. To make

Lieutenant-Colonel Chamberlin, the "Hero of Eccles Hill," sporting the insignia of Companion of the Order of St. Michael and St. George, and carrying his sword of honour. The sword is on display at the Bytown Museum in Ottawa.

matters worse, it came during the lunch hour, while many of Chamberlin's men were off "procuring meals" at nearby farmhouses.

The Fenians, who according to some accounts now numbered over 600 men, suddenly began their first advance in a loose column of some 200 with a small advance guard. Chamberlin was left with hardly more than 50 men, who opened fire as soon as the Fenian advance rushed onto Canadian soil.

With their first volley, the Canadians killed one man and wounded several others. The Fenians halted, wavered, partially rallied again, and then, overcome by the well-sustained and well-directed fire from the Canadians, broke line and ran—some retreating to safety on the American side, others seeking refuge behind trees, houses and stone fences along the road. From the safety of their shelter, the invaders kept up a desultory fire, but their reserve of about 400 men never joined in the action. Chamberlin described what happened:

The fire of the Fenian column, while formed as such, was very ill-directed, sometimes more resembling a *feu de joie* than anything else. Hardly a shot came near us, till after shelter had been gained by the enemy.

A few hours later, just before dusk, the Canadians advanced to the boundary line and drove the lurking Fenians in "full and even ludicrous flight" across the border. The

Dominion's Reserve Militia, was in Toronto when news of the crisis came. From there, he rushed to an area of the front just south of Montreal near his birthplace. This position was considered particularly strategic because there, at a high point of land called Eccles Hill, Fenians had succeeded in establishing a

VOL. I.—No. 1.   MONTREAL, SAMEDI, 1er JANVIER, 1870.   ABONNEMENT $2.50. Par Numéro 5 Centins.

stronghold in a raid four years earlier and were likely to do so again. Lieutenant-Colonel Chamberlin took charge of a small Canadian force outnumbered by some six to one.

Despite these odds, the hastily assembled Canadian troops repulsed the raid and drove the

invaders back across the border, effectively ending the Fenians' dreams of Canadian conquest. Except for a minor skirmish two days later, Fenians all along the border withdrew once and for all.

Chamberlin's financial distress was over. Within two weeks, the new Hero of Eccles Hill resigned his seat in Parliament to accept the appointment as Queen's Printer; a week later, he and Agnes Dunbar Moodie FitzGibbon were married before a "large and fashionable assembly." Chamberlin remained in office for over 21 years, which makes him the country's longest serving Queen's Printer.

Canadians were so elated that their commanding officers were hard-pressed to keep them from pursuing the retreating enemy into United States territory. Chamberlin's men suffered no casualties, but two dozen or more Fenians were dead or wounded, and their commander was taken into custody by a United States Marshall at the scene.

Her Majesty's subjects responded to news of the victory with jubilant, patriotic fervour. Canadian newspapers carried detailed accounts of the engagement. George Edward Desbarats' *Canadian Illustrated News*, which had sent a special artist to the frontier, pronounced that the scuffle might "fairly be entitled a 'battle' from the important consequences of the victory achieved, if not from the actual slaughter." The magazine gloated that the Irish Republican Army's acronym, I.R.A., stood for "I Ran Away."

Prince Arthur, who was in Canada, travelled to Eccles Hill to review the troops and congratulate them on their victory. Later, a small monument was erected at the site.

Lieutenant-Colonels Chamberlin and Smith and two other officers were named Companions of the Order of St. Michael and St. George by Queen Victoria. Not to be outdone, 293 prominent Ottawa citizens each subscribed one dollar for the purchase of a "sword of honour" for Lieutenant-Colonel Chamberlin, "in appreciation of his gallantry in repelling the invasion of marauders from the neighboring republic." The sword was presented in the Senate chambers, with the Governor General presiding.

Within days, the Hero of Eccles Hill became the new Queen's Printer for Canada. Though he retired from the militia, Chamberlin continued, by permission, to use his military title for the rest of his life.

Palsied the arm that forges yokes,
At my fat contracts squintin',
An' withered be the nose that pokes
Inter the gov'ment printin'!

The Inland Printer,
on the state of the
contract system in Canada

he 1869 Queen's Printer's Act finally put an end to the lucrative private monopoly on the printing of the *Canada Gazette* and the *Statutes*. It also aimed to reform the system by which the executive branches of government were formerly allowed to set the rates paid for departmental printing and to distribute the work according to the dictates of patronage. Now all printing for government departments, as well as that previously covered by the royal patent, was to be done under five-year contracts on the same basis as parliamentary printing. However, under the new contract system, the reforms stipulated by the Act were, at best, only partially successful.

For one thing, the system continued as a mixed one, since the new legislation failed to centralize all government printing and binding under one head. The Joint Committee on Printing, with help from its clerk, Henry Hartney, continued independently to supervise the separate contracts for parliamentary printing and binding, while under the new Act, the Queen's Printer was in charge only of work performed for the departments, and for the *Canada Gazette* and the *Statutes*. Because there was no single central authority over government printing, it was nearly impossible for administrators to supervise the separate contracts effectively. The Committee and the Queen's Printer, who each supervised different contracts signed with the same firm, sometimes ordered separate copies of identical reports and documents. Almost immediately, the cost-reducing purpose of the contract system was undermined because the very first contractor took advantage of this unnecessary duplication of work to increase profits.

Another great weakness of the Act was that it addressed, but failed to resolve, the question of patronage. Though the new law required government departments to order their printing and binding under the contract supervised by the Queen's Printer, section 7 of the Act established an exception to this rule. In theory, the exception was intended to allow depart-ments to give confidential printing to other print shops and to pay for it at higher, "confidential rates." But in practice, it gave politicians licence and exposed them to the same pressures to distribute the government's patronage that had existed before the passing of the Act. Before long, ways were found to circumvent the Queen's Printer's Act, resulting in political and financial embarrassments greater than ever before.

As early as 1859, the Joint Committee on Printing had suggested that the establishment of a government print shop and bindery would solve such problems. But at that time, the Queen's Printer still held letters patent from the Crown, and public opinion was so opposed to any form of government competition with private enterprise that the notion was not taken seriously. Not until some 25 years later, after the weaknesses of the contract system as it then existed had placed the government in a completely untenable position, would the establishment of in-house printing capability finally be recognized as a necessity.

But in 1869, the announcement of contracts to be awarded under the Queen's Printer's authority created exceptional circumstances. For the first time, large quantities of printing, binding and paper formerly purchased as patronage, or supplied under a royal commission, were to be procured under contracts awarded on the basis of competitive tenders. For the printing, three separate contracts were drawn up: one for departmental printing, another for printing of the *Statutes* and a third for the *Canada*

Gazette. The departmental printing contract was intended to centralize work that formerly had been distributed to printers from one end of the Dominion to the other. It required the successful bidder to furnish correct proofs of each order and to be ready to deliver work at short notice. On forms and other matter kept standing in type, the contractor was permitted to charge full composition once a year.

The printing of the *Canada Gazette* and the *Statutes*, formerly executed under the Queen's Printer's commission, had always been more expensive than ordinary printing, partly because of the legal necessity for absolute accuracy. The printed *Statutes* had to be exact to copy—any mistake rendered the contractor liable to reprint the sheet at his own expense—and delivered, complete, to the binder within six weeks of the close of each session. The contractor had to maintain sufficient staff and equipment, not only to handle large quantities of urgent work on short notice, but also because the *Canada Gazette*, regardless of its size, still had to be complete and delivered each Saturday, the day of issue. Here too, the printer was held responsible for any error or deviation from copy, and for any issues lost in the mail through incorrect addressing or packaging. Unlike the Queen's Printers of earlier years, the contractor was not permitted to sell extra copies of the *Canada Gazette* or the *Statutes*, nor was the firm entitled to profits from paid advertisements appearing in the government's official newspaper. In addition,

the contractor was required to provide safe storage for printing paper, which was delivered in quantity under a separate paper-supply contract. A contract was also drawn up for binding the *Statutes*, requiring the bookbinder to maintain a large establishment, since the firm was required to deliver bound volumes at the rate of at least 2,000 per week.

Firms in Toronto, Georgetown, Ottawa and Montreal submitted tenders, and a few days after the Queen's Printer's Act officially came into force on October 1, 1869, all the contracts were signed. Isaac Boulton Taylor, proprietor of *The Ottawa Citizen* and the new printer to Parliament, was awarded all three printing contracts; the contract for binding of the *Statutes* went to Robert Hunter, George Maclean Rose and François Lemieux, of Hunter, Rose and Company; while James Cotton of Ottawa won the right to supply printing paper for the *Canada Gazette* and *Statutes*. At first, no contracts were issued for the supply of departmental printing paper or for departmental binding requirements. The paper was supplied by the government's recently established stationery office, while binding services were purchased from various firms at fixed prices determined by the Queen's Printer.

As expected, under the stress of competition, and knowing that they would receive the entire quantity of government work for a five-year period, the bidders had offered their services at much lower prices than those formerly demanded. In fact, competition was so keen that unprecedented prices were quoted—prices which many feared were too low to recover the cost

The Parliamentary East Block, as it appeared
in the 1870s

of production.

For the printing contracts in particular, the successful tender was extremely low. Isaac Boulton Taylor proposed to charge the departments only 12½ cents per 1,000 ems of composition. The charge for the *Canada Gazette* was 15 cents, with an additional five cent charge for each re-insertion of old matter. For the *Statutes*, Taylor offered to set a page of type measuring 2,126 ems for 30 cents. For presswork, he quoted a charge of 15 cents per token of 250 or more impressions and even offered a discount on departmental orders of over 5,000 copies.

In comparison, George Edward Desbarats had charged the government 50 cents per 1,000 ems of composition, and per token of presswork. At Taylor's prices, the *Statutes* would cost less than one third of what they had cost under the royal patent. In fact, whereas in 1869 the government had paid Desbarats $21,500, or nearly 99 cents per volume, to print the session's *Statutes*; in 1870 Taylor received only $5,250 for the edition, or about 27 cents for a similarly-sized volume.

An astonished Prime Minister Macdonald asked George Edward Desbarats, the recently appointed Queen's Printer, about the discrepancy between his former rates and those now offered by the contractors. But Desbarats remained unconcerned:

The lowest wages for compositors are now 25 c. per 1,000 ems. If anyone chooses to undertake it [the printing of statutes] at 14 c., and pay interest on capital, wear and tear, rent, fuel, light, proof-readers, book-keepers, taxes, &c., besides, he is free to do it, and make money by it, if he can. Time will tell its tale.

Desbarats' words must surely have come back to haunt the Prime Minister. On the face of it, the contract system seemed to have ushered in an era of much lower costs; but in fact it had also introduced an entirely different set of problems.

The Queen's Printer's Branch

When Brown Chamberlin retired from politics and the militia to assume what *The Dominion Illustrated* called "the quiet, unobtrusive duties of a civil servant," he moved from the offices of the House of Commons to those of the Department of the Secretary of State in the East Block. An 1870 amendment to the Queen's Printer's Act made him an officer of that department, which then consisted of five branches, with a total of 20 employees. In his own branch, the Queen's Printer had a clerk, T.H. Hodgins, and a messenger, Auguste Potvin, to help him.

Chamberlin probably did find the new job "unobtrusive" compared to the excitement of his recent military activities. Judging from his reports, however, the duties were anything but quiet. Upon his arrival, he found the work had fallen drastically behind in the two months since George Desbarats' resignation. Hodgins had been able to conduct only the urgent work the departments required day by day. It took a year before the methods of ordering work, of accounting and of auditing were systematized, and before another clerk was added to the staff. This was William Gliddon, a practical printer and binder, who had come to Canada from Devon, England, in 1833. Gliddon was destined to become the future Public Printing and Stationery Department's first chief accountant.

As government departments became accustomed to new rules for ordering their printing and binding, the number of requisitions received by the Queen's Printer rapidly increased. In 1870, the office processed about 125 requisitions each month; a year later that number had nearly doubled. Chamberlin handled most purchases for the departments situated in Ottawa and for their "outside" offices located throughout Ontario and Quebec. In his report for 1871, Chamberlin described the steps required for placing each of these orders, giving some idea of the amount of work the tiny staff turned out. Their feat was particularly impressive, as all the records were painstakingly written out in longhand and the government work day was only six hours long.

Departmental requisitions for printing, ruling or binding were sent to the Queen's Printer by the deputy ministers or their designated officers. The Queen's Printer then recorded their orders and issued his own requisitions to the various contractors for printing and binding, and to the Stationery Office or to the contractor for paper. The requisite paper was shipped, in turn, to the printer's establishment. The Queen's Printer was also responsible for supervising jobs during production and inspecting and counting the finished work, which was always returned first to his office. If completed according to requisition, it was repacked and hauled to the offices of the client department. Requisitions, departmental receipts and delivery slips all had to be recorded and, before the contractors' bills were paid, they too were checked,

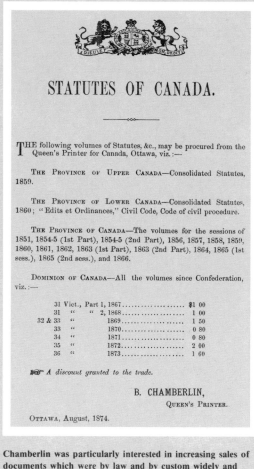

Chamberlin was particularly interested in increasing sales of documents which were by law and by custom widely and gratuitously distributed throughout the country. In 1874, he managed to sell 197 English and 3 French copies of the session's *Statutes*.

registered, and sent to the respective departments and to the Clerk of Contingencies.

In 1871, nearly 70,000 volumes of books, pamphlets and maps were printed, bound, ruled or mounted, and nearly 5.5 million forms were printed or ruled. The following year, Senator James Cox Aikins, the Secretary of State, reported:

The constant supervision of the printing and binding for the several Departments, and the uniform audit of the accounts for those services as performed under contracts at a schedule of prices, tend alike to economy and uniformity of work and price—both satisfactory results. The system of the office has been so far perfected that now the cost of every detail of every job can at once be ascertained, and the account promptly closed. The basis for future contracts or other arrangements, derivable from the registered statistics of the office, will always hereafter be forthcoming when needed.

Departmental printing comprised only a fraction of the responsibilities of the office. It also supervised the printing, binding and distribution of the *Canada Gazette* and of the *Statutes*. Requisitions for advertisements in the *Gazette* were sent from the departments and from other agencies or individuals. These were treated in the manner described above. In addition, fees for subscriptions and for advertisements had to be collected and accounts had to be kept.

For each session, between 15,000 and 22,000 copies of the *Statutes* were printed, bound and distributed under the supervision of the Queen's Printer. Careful records of distribution were maintained because the

The Queen's Printer reported to Parliament through the Secretary of State, a portfolio which Senator James Cox Aikins held from 1869-1873, and from 1878-1880.

Queen's Printer was still required by law to submit a detailed report to Parliament each session.

The acts issued under the imprint of the Queen's Printer were law, as they are

today, and were recognized as authentic in the courts. Responsibility for their accuracy was then, as now, a serious matter and demanded a great deal of personal attention on Chamberlin's part.

Outside Ontario and Quebec most federal government offices purchased their printing and stationery locally, at whatever prices could be arranged with local printers and stationers. But beginning in 1877, offices in New Brunswick, Nova Scotia, Prince Edward Island, Manitoba and British Columbia began to order printing from the Queen's Printer, and stationery from the government's stationery office.

The change brought additional work to the two offices, and additional savings to the government. At contract rates, much lower prices were paid than those that had been charged by local suppliers; and besides, the Queen's Printer and Superintendent of Stationery were able to exercise more effective control over the quality and quantity of work ordered.

The Post Office was a major departmental consumer of printing and stationery supplies. A comparison of that department's purchases under the local system with those under the contract provides a graphic illustration of just how much cheaper goods were when purchased through central Ottawa offices. In 1876, the Post Office had spent over $11,000 in New Brunswick and over $15,000 in Nova Scotia; but after supplies began to arrive from Ottawa, the Department's expenses in each of those provinces plunged to just over $3,000.

The Government Stationery Office

The conditions that led to the creation of a government stationery office in 1868 were similar to those that led to the passing of the Queen's Printer's Act in 1869. For many years, members of the Opposition and newspapers had complained about the way the government purchased and dispensed printing paper and stationery supplies. At the time, each department usually bought its own stationery, at whatever prices could be negotiated with the Queen's Printer or with other suppliers. The costs were charged to the government's contingencies budget. This system had resulted in the same problems—escalating costs, unsuitable or unnecessary purchases and other extravagances—that plagued the procurement of printing and binding. Inevitably, there were accusations of mismanagement and political patronage, which eventually became impossible to ignore.

A typical incident involved the Crown Lands Office, which in 1861 purchased over $11,000 worth of stationery supplies from S.B. Foote, the proprietor of the *Morning Chronicle*, an official government newspaper in Quebec. According to the Assistant Commissioner of Crown Lands, this was enough paper for at least ten years; and according to testimony before the Standing Committee for Public Accounts, when the paper was delivered and stored in the Department's attic, the public and political imagination was fired by the possibility that such hoarding might cause the building to collapse. Further inquiry revealed that Foote's prices were considerably higher than those charged by the Queen's Printer—many were double, triple, even five and six times higher than the prices that the Legislative Assembly paid for stationery.

Shortly after Confederation, a committee of the Privy Council found that such unnecessary expenditures were by no means unusual. Most departments bought more stationery than was needed, and paid higher prices for it than did the legislature. Purchases of steel pens in particular caused a minor scandal. Parliament paid less than $1.80 for a dozen, while the departments paid as much as $2.50, and in the first year after Confederation, purchased $1,500 worth—more than 600 dozen steel pens. Perhaps because steel-nibbed pens were just coming into vogue (and because many clerks still wrote with the old-style quill), members of the Opposition seized upon the pens as a symbol of government extravagance and waste.

Scandalous as the situation seemed, the departments were not so much to blame as the system itself. Deputy heads, who authorized all purchases, did not necessarily have the expertise to assess requirements, compare prices and quality, or make the most economical choices. On the other hand, the Accountant of Contingencies, who automatically paid requisitions forwarded to him from the departments, had no authority to decide what should be purchased or from whom. Even where no patronage was involved, procedures did not allow for control or meaningful audit of purchases.

When the Accountant of Contingencies, Thomas Ross, first proposed the establishment of a government stationery office, the idea was eagerly adopted by Finance Minister John Rose. On May 22, 1868, "An Act to regulate and restrict the Contingent Charges of the Departments of the Public Service and to establish a Stationery Office" received royal assent.

For the first time, a chief clerk, who was an expert in the paper trade, was to buy printing paper and stationery in quantity for the entire civil service while negotiating for fair prices. Also, this clerk, working from a central office, would maintain a regular inventory and prepare detailed records for submission to Parliament.

Interestingly, the Act also empowered the Chief Clerk to procure departmental printing and binding, a duty which was reassigned to the Queen's Printer a year later, before the new office was actually organized. According to an early draft of the Queen's Printer's Act, the government had also considered making the Queen's Printer responsible for procuring departmental printing paper and stationery, but this idea was dropped before the Act became law in June 1869. Consequently, even though the function was closely related to the work of the Queen's Printer, departmental printing paper and stationery were purchased and supplied by a separate government stationery office.

Even before a chief was appointed, the Finance Minister obtained Privy Council approval for stocking the office with a year's supply of stationery imported directly from Her Majesty's Stationery Office (HMSO) in London. Many of the finer papers and specialty stationery items were not yet manufactured in the Dominion, and purchasing these from a Canadian firm usually meant purchasing from an importer rather than from a producer, and having to pay the importer's profits. Until the Stationery Office could enter into contracts with foreign manufacturers, HMSO had promised to supply the Dominion for a five percent commission over its own rates.

As it turned out, it was fortunate that these preparations were under way when Desbarats' establishment on Sparks Street was destroyed by fire. Shortly afterwards, James Young, a skilled bookbinder from Scotland, who had been the foreman of the Desbarats bindery, joined the civil service to organize the new office. By May 1869, three months after the fire, Young was supplying local government departments. By January 1870, he was also supplying some stationery to the "outside service," as departmental offices located away from the capital were called.

The Stationery Office proved to be a reliable source of supply and demonstrated a notable potential for reducing expenditures. From May 1869 to June 1870, Young purchased supplies worth about $30,000 and issued goods to the various departments worth about $20,000. Under his supervision, a sufficient number of those embarrassing steel pens that had cost $1,500 in 1867 were obtained for only $405.

Each year, as Canada and the civil service grew, the departments used more stationery. In 1873, Young issued goods worth nearly $38,000. He also maintained tight control over every detail of expenditure, large or small. With dogged determination, he managed for years to protect his reforms from the incursions of party patronage and "muckery."

Though government policy was to "buy Canadian" if goods of Canadian manufacture could be had, Young continued to import between one half and two thirds of the year's stationery supplies from England. This need to import was probably the major source of difficulty in keeping costs low. Since departments submitted their estimates of anticipated requirements only once a year, Young was often forced to meet sudden unforeseen demands by purchasing locally from importers or by carrying more stock than was ideally necessary.

In 1875, Young travelled to England and there negotiated lower prices with manufacturers of fine papers. As a direct result, prices for many stationery items were afterwards much reduced. Even at the lower 1876 prices, the Stationery Office recorded purchases of over $54,000, issues totalling about $56,500, and a profit of more than $1,000 on the year's business. About half of the goods issued went to the Queen's Printer, and the rest went directly to the departments.

James Young was a skilled craftsman who also embodied all the traditional ideals of the old-fashioned civil servant. His reforms were widely publicized, earning him praise within the service and from the public. In 1878, *The Ottawa Free Press* described the Stationery Office as:

. . . the means of saving many thousands of dollars annually—some estimate it from seventy-five to one hundred thousand dollars—to the Crown, upon the old rates paid to Desbarats and Derbishire and others.

A close association always existed between the Queen's Printer's Branch and the Stationery Office. The Queen's Printer was, after all, the office's largest customer, for it was in response to Chamberlin's requisitions that the Stationery Office supplied contractors with printing paper for the departments' books, pamphlets and forms. In his first annual report for 1870, Chamberlin reported that Young had helped him establish fixed rates to be paid for the departmental binding. And after 1873, when the Stationery Office was transferred from the Finance Department to the Secretary of State, it was located in the East Block near the Queen's Printer's Branch because of this close relationship. In 1886, the Stationery Office became a branch of the Department of Public Printing and Stationery.

The lowest wages for compositors are now 25 c. per 1,000 ems. If anyone chooses to undertake it [the printing of statutes] *at 14 c., and pay interest on capital, wear and tear, rent, fuel, light, proof-readers, book-keepers, taxes, &c., besides, he is free to do it, and make money by it, if he can. Time will tell its tale.*

George Edward Desbarats,
Queen's Printer, 1869

n 1869, Isaac Boulton Taylor was able to offer the lowest tenders for the printing contracts under the Queen's Printer's supervision on the strength of his five-year contract for the parliamentary printing, which he had won from the previous printers a few months earlier. Taylor's extremely low bid for Parliament's work had already provoked considerable discussion in the House. The Joint Committee on Printing at first rejected the tender, fearing that Taylor's prices were so far below cost that it would be impossible for him to carry out the work. Instead, the Committee wanted Parliament to renew the contract with Hunter, Rose and Company, the firm that had been doing the parliamentary printing and binding since 1860, and suggested that this would be safer and cheaper than a recurrence of the 1860 incident, in which parliamentary contractor Samuel Thompson had overextended himself and failed within the first year of his contract.

However, public opinion strongly favoured awarding the contract to the lowest bidder, and at this time, the Bill for abolishing the Queen's Printer's commission was already before the House. Unwilling to give the appearance of undermining reform by rejecting the lowest bid for its own printing, Parliament ultimately decided in Taylor's favour. Without the parliamentary printing contract, Hunter, Rose was unable to compete with Taylor's prices for departmental printing. As a result, the parliamentary printing contractor also became the departmental contractor.

Hunter, Rose, the former parliamentary printing company which had been awarded only the relatively small contracts for bookbinding, soon withdrew and closed its Ottawa plant. After this, with all the government printing in the hands of one printer, there was not enough work in the capital to support another large

printing operation. Because Desbarats' establishment had already been destroyed by fire, no print shop in Ottawa besides Taylor's had sufficient capacity to perform the government's work.

Taylor proposed to charge the government a lower rate than had ever been asked before. The rate charged by Hunter, Rose, of 28 cents per 1,000 ems of composition, was less than half what the Queen's Printer had charged under the patent. Even at that rate, the company could not have received a profitable return; yet Taylor was proposing to halve Hunter, Rose's rate again.

Taylor based his calculations on the practice, common among former parliamentary printers, of subsidizing rates. One way of doing this was to make up for the low prices of composition by charging the various government departments for it a second time.

This invisible subsidy was common in the printers' charges for the annual reports presented to Parliament. Under the parliamentary contract, the number of copies printed and paid for did not exceed the number required for the use of the members of the two Houses. In most cases, the departments ordered another edition for their own general distribution, and paid for it separately. The parliamentary printer customarily charged departments not just for the extra press runs, but also for composition, even though the pages did not have to be typeset again. Departments could order printing anywhere, but whether or not they went to the parliamentary printer, they would have to pay for the composition of their own copies.

When Taylor calculated his quotation, he had assumed that he would be paid double for the composition of all the large annual reports. This had been the practice when George E. Desbarats was the Queen's Printer. At that time, Desbarats, seeing that the cost to the government would be no more than would be paid to the contractor for departmental work if he happened to be someone other than the parliamentary printer, allowed Taylor's charge. As an experienced master printer, Desbarats undoubtedly knew that Taylor could not otherwise fulfil his contractual responsibilities.

During the session of 1870, the Joint Committee on the Printing of Parliament first became aware of the double payments under Taylor's two contracts. It promptly passed a resolution that this double charge should not be allowed, and recommended that departments order the number of copies they required under the parliamentary contract, from committee Clerk Henry Hartney. Even though Taylor's system of double charges clearly wiped out the potential savings under the new contract system, this resolution was passed only with difficulty, by a narrow majority of committee members. This, and the fact that Desbarats had allowed the charges without question, shows how prevalent and generally accepted was the practice of double charges.

Taylor remonstrated with the government on the grounds that the Joint Committee's action had undermined the very foundation on which his tender was based; but the Committee, by a vote of eleven to nine, reaffirmed the principle that double charges should no longer be allowed. With the government's consent, Taylor took his claim to the Court of Queen's Bench, but lost his suit on a technicality.

Unfortunately for Taylor, the Committee's action, leading to his loss of the double composition upon which he depended to make his contracts remunerative, was only one of his many troubles. The early 1870s were fraught with economic turmoil, with constant increases in the cost of living and, consequently, with much labour unrest. No sooner were Taylor's five-year contracts signed than the prices of labour and materials began a steady upward climb. The first cost increase came early in 1870, when the printers obtained a raise in their rates.

Taylor, who had contracted to deliver 1,000 ems of composition for as little as 12½ cents, was now obliged to pay his compositors 27 cents, or more than twice as much, to do the work. At the same time, employees paid by the day, who formerly earned seven dollars a week, now received nine. These were just the first of many increases. Under the terms of his contract, and without the double charge for annual reports, Taylor clearly could not survive for long. The first signs of trouble soon appeared in Parliament. Only weeks after Hunter, Rose closed its Ottawa establishment, members began complaining about delays in the printing of bills.

Taylor's excuse was that the parliamentary and departmental work were too heavy a load, especially when the departments sometimes insisted that their work should take precedence. Two of his presses were shut down, and he could do no more for Parliament.

The Joint Committee on Printing would have to look elsewhere for a solution.

Theoretically, the parliamentary printing contractor was required to have sufficient presses and enough staff available to ensure that Parliament would never be inconvenienced. But since Taylor was not even earning enough to pay his compositors, maintaining the extra staff and machinery that would have been required to meet such emergencies was entirely beyond his budget. That Parliament's consideration of legislation should be delayed because of the printer was a serious matter, but with Hunter, Rose out of the city, no print shop in Ottawa was capable of making up the deficiency.

A delay in the delivery of the *Statutes* for the 1872 session led to another embarrassing incident. Though the printer was required to deliver copies six weeks after Parliament prorogued, the *Statutes* did not arrive in the Maritimes until six *months* after the end of the session. In the meantime, smallpox had struck in Nova Scotia, and it was claimed in the Senate that authorities had been forced to respond without the benefit of a new quarantine law. The volumes of the *Statutes* for the Maritimes were sent to the provincial secretaries for local deliveries, and Secretary of State Senator Aikins tried to place the blame for most of the delay on this system of distribution. The printing had been only slightly delayed, he claimed, because of the size of the volume. Although the Minister of Agriculture had also distributed the Quarantine Act in pamphlet form, apparently no one from Nova Scotia had ever seen it.

Whether the fault lay with the printer or with the distribution system, the delay caused a major embarrassment. And the whole discussion also publicized another serious problem: the French edition of the 1872 *Statutes* was even later, having been delivered to the senators' offices three months later than the English.

The more desperate Taylor's financial situation became, the more grounds for complaint he gave Parliament and the departments. Much of the printing was not only late, it was also decidedly inferior to the quality stipulated by Taylor's contracts. Officers of the government were generally obliged to accept it, either because the work was required in a rush or, according to Chamberlin, because it was "as good as the prices paid for it."

In December 1872, Taylor's printers began backing their demands for further pay increases with threats of a strike on the eve of the reconvening of Parliament. Taylor petitioned the government for financial relief, claiming that his employees' wage demands, which were to take effect on the first day of January 1873, increased the price of composition by 40 percent over what he paid in 1869 when he bid for the printing contracts. The wages of women and children, who were used to provide cheap labour as press feeders, folders and stitchers, had risen even more, by as much as 100 to 200 percent. It was rumoured that Taylor was on the verge of closing his establishment and abandoning his contracts.

To avert the contemplated strike and a potential crisis, Henry Hartney, Clerk to the Joint Committee

on Printing, recommended
to the Minister of Justice
that the government should
pay the cost of increased
wages week by week until
Parliament reconvened and
could consider the matter.
Accordingly, the Privy
Council granted Taylor a
total of $8,000 in advances
while Queen's Printer
Chamberlin was asked to
conduct an inquiry to
establish the veracity of the
contractor's claims.

In spite of these
monetary advances, Taylor's
finances had reached a state of crisis by the time
Parliament reconvened in March 1873. When the
Court of the Queen's Bench decided against him in
the matter of the double charges, the contractor
immediately notified Parliament that without additional compensation, he had no alternative but to
suspend operations altogether. Taylor could no longer
survive the heavy daily losses sustained from not being
paid for double composition, combined with the
unexpected increase in the cost of labour.

In Taylor's defense it can be said that his low
prices were only partly to blame for all these problems.
Economic conditions were such that many long-term
contractors were running into serious difficulties. The
cost of materials had increased even more than the

cost of labour, and James Cotton, the contractor for
paper for the *Canada Gazette* and the *Statutes*, had
long since withdrawn, "finding it impracticable to
fulfill his contract to the satisfaction of the Government
at the prices for which he tendered." New tenders
had to be invited, and a new contract, at higher rates,
was signed with Barber Brothers of Georgetown, the
paper manufacturers who had formerly made the
paper George Edward Desbarats furnished to Parliament. It is probable that, even if Hunter, Rose had
won the parliamentary printing contract at their slightly
higher rates, this company too would have been forced
to ask the Joint Committee on Printing for more money.
In fact Hunter, Rose did approach the provincial
government in Toronto for an advance and, according
to Queen's Printer Chamberlin, were getting twice as
much as Taylor for that government's composition
and presswork.

Nevertheless, if the early 1870s were difficult for
all contractors, they were ruinous for Taylor. He gave
up all his other printing assignments, including his
newspaper, *The Ottawa Citizen*, and was even forced
to sell large portions of his private property. Still, he
found himself without the means to pay his workers,
who were constantly threatening to strike. Having
exhausted $8,000 in advances, the contractor proposed
to the Joint Committee on Printing that he be reim-
bursed for his loss of the double charge for the
departmental reports, and also for the direct losses
he was sustaining as a result of rising wages.

Taylor maintained that overall, he was losing at
least 58 cents on every dollar of printing. While some

members of the Committee on Printing agreed with this estimate, Chamberlin reported otherwise. A survey the Queen's Printer conducted revealed varying rates of inflation in Canadian cities. But in Montreal, where conditions in the printing trades most closely resembled those in Ottawa, leading printers had experienced increases averaging only 27½ percent. The Committee eventually agreed with Chamberlin, and recommended that Taylor be granted a 27 percent increase on the parliamentary printing contract prices. It refused, however, to reimburse him for the loss of the double composition charges for annual reports.

The Committee's report caused a minor sensation in the House. Rather than grant Taylor his increase, some members of the Opposition recommended relieving him of his contract. They charged that Taylor had tendered at merely nominal rates in order to get Hunter, Rose and Company out of the city; that he had never intended to meet the terms of his contract; and that he had planned from the start to get his rates increased later. They even produced a telegram from Hunter, Rose in Toronto, offering to complete the session's work at Taylor's prices.

The government's "desire to do justice" carried the day, and Taylor won his increase. Short of accepting major interruptions in the work, Parliament really had little choice but to afford the contractor some measure of relief, since he would otherwise have closed his establishment permanently. But in doing so, they were forced to compromise the tendering principle and, once the idea of altering fixed contract prices was introduced, the contracts supervised by the Queen's Printer were also renegotiated. In June, Taylor obtained an increase of 27 percent to the departmental contract rates; in July, his rates for printing the *Canada Gazette* and the *Statutes* were also increased.

All of Taylor's sacrifices, and even the government's last-minute concessions, came too late to prevent the worrisome interruption of work. By the

Printers' Inklings: A Family Tradition

An account of one of the labour disputes that was partly to blame for Isaac Boulton Taylor's problems with government printing has survived in local union records. This is of interest because they mention the names of two prominent strikers whose families later became important in connection with the Printing Bureau.

During the strike, two feisty printers from *The Ottawa Citizen* were arrested for leaving their employment without due notice. They were convicted, and each was fined one dollar plus one dollar court costs—an amount equal to nearly two days' pay. The first striker was Andrew Pelton, father of Lorne Andrew Pelton, future long-time bindery foreman at the Printing Bureau. The other was William Armstrong, the first of four generations of Armstrong printers involved in government printing. William's son, Frank Joseph Armstrong, became one of the Printing Bureau's original compositors and one of the first printers to operate the linotype machines there. William's grandson, Gordon Victor Armstrong, began as a hand compositor at the Printing Bureau, and remained for over 47 years, retiring as a senior officer in 1967. Continuing the family tradition is William's great-grandson Brian Armstrong, who works in Printing Services' Statistics Canada Plant. Thanks to William Armstrong's strike action, we have a record of at least one family whose members have served as government printers for as long as Canada has had a Queen's Printer.

end of July, Taylor's printers were out on strike. They joined other Ottawa journeymen printers who stayed off the job for over two months.

Taylor closed his establishment briefly and then broke the strike by re-opening with a staff of printers from England. Since the new workers lacked experience in parliamentary work, more trouble and confusion were added to the embarrassment of increased costs. Both Henry Hartney, the Clerk of the Joint Committee on the Printing of Parliament, and Brown Chamberlin complained of serious delays and inferior

work. The French portion of the printing particularly suffered, since Taylor could no longer find qualified French-language compositors in Ottawa. In March 1874, Hartney reported that the contractor had finally sent the work to printers in Montreal, and that the arrears were gradually being made up.

Taylor somehow managed to carry through, though he never really recovered. It must have been a relief to all concerned when his contracts finally expired in July and September 1874.

If this principle of centralization is carried out to its entirety, then our people will have to go to Ottawa, or the United States, to earn their living.

The Printer's Miscellany,
Saint John, New Brunswick, 1876

n theory, the Queen's Printer's Act of 1869 reformed the way government departments purchased printing services; in practice, the reform proved difficult to implement.

Five years after the Act was passed, the public was still clamouring for an end to the enormous waste that resulted from the practice of handing departmental printing work, often labelled as "confidential," to political friends of the party in power. Outside the

CANADIAN Illustrated News

SINGLE COPIES TEN CENTS.
$4 PER YEAR IN ADVANCE.

MONTREAL, SATURDAY, MARCH 13, 1875.

Vol. XI.—No. 11.

THAT INEXORABLE HANSARD!

DISTRACTED MEMBER:—Well, I declare, after all the trouble I took to write out a splendid speech for my constituents to read here, that stupid county paper of theirs publishing it as I spoke it, word for word! The *Hansard* must have got there before my manuscript!

This cartoon appeared after Parliament finally decided to publish an official record of its debates in 1875. Strong supporters of official reporting, like the *Canadian Illustrated News*, suspected, but could not prove, political bias in the reports of parliamentary debates which were printed in the newspapers. Another serious objection to the newspaper reports was that speeches delivered in French received only cursory coverage, even from the French-language press, which was more concerned with proceedings in the Quebec legislature than in the House of Commons.

Because of these shortcomings, the publication of an official record, such as Great Britain's *Hansard*, was often debated in Parliament, under both the Province of Canada, and the Dominion. Private firms published several unofficial volumes of debates, but an official record had been tried only once. In 1865, Hunter, Rose printed Parliament's lengthy debate on confederation—a project which turned into such an enormous undertaking that it may have had more to do with the members' reluctance to institute a printed record than the fear of impartial reporting suggested by the cartoon.

provinces of Ontario and Quebec, the Act's reforms were not implemented at all. And even in the two provinces where the reforms were partially implemented, government departments continued to distribute much printing through patronage, instead of obtaining it under contract through the Queen's Printer. In the Maritimes, the so-called "local" system remained in effect: no printing whatsoever was purchased through the Queen's Printer in Ottawa.

In 1874, MacLean, Roger and Company, the firm which succeeded Isaac Boulton Taylor as official contractor for departmental and parliamentary printing, added its protests against patronage and confidential printing. No sooner was the departmental printing contract signed than the company notified the Secretary of State that it held the right to perform all government printing. Principals Alexander MacLean and John Charles Roger contended that departmental printing carried out in New Brunswick, Nova Scotia and Prince Edward Island by rival printers constituted a breach of contract.

But despite objections from the public and the contractor, the government did little to reduce the steady flow of lucrative printing assignments to newspapers and job-printing offices around the country. Its reluctance is understandable in light of the printing trade's reaction to the Queen's Printer's Act. *The Printer's Miscellany*, a New Brunswick trade journal, ran a series of articles protesting the reform. "If this principle of centralization is carried out in its entirety," the monthly commented in 1876, "then our people will have to go to Ottawa, or the United States, to earn their living." According to the journal, had the work been distributed through the tendering process, instead of being used by politicians to accomplish their own ends, it could have been obtained as cheaply in Saint John or Halifax as in Ottawa.

Nevertheless, under the so-called "local" system, work was generally distributed on the basis of patronage, which resulted in many abuses. A particularly painful scandal occurred in 1874, after a new Liberal government switched the patronage of the Post Office printing from newspapers affiliated with the Conservatives to newspapers espousing the Liberal cause. An anonymous letter in the *Montreal Gazette*, charged that *The Freeman*, a New Brunswick paper owned and edited by the Speaker of the House, Timothy Warren Anglin, was among those that had obtained government contracts for Post Office printing. The writer charged that this violated not only the Independence of Parliament Act, but also the new law under which departmental printing was supposed to be performed under a contract supervised by the Queen's Printer.

The rumours and allegations were confirmed in March 1877, when the Select Standing Committee on Public Accounts laid vouchers before the House showing that the Speaker's paper had indeed received printing contracts worth over $20,000 between 1874 and 1876. *The Freeman* had not actually done the printing, but had subcontracted it to another printing office.

DEBATES

OF THE

HOUSE OF COMMONS,

OF THE

DOMINION OF CANADA,

REPORTED AND EDITED BY A. M. BURGESS.

VOL I.—SESSION 1875.

Ottawa :

PRINTED BY C. W. MITCHELL, "FREE PRESS" OFFICE, ELGIN STREET,

1875.

This edition of *Debates* is the first official *Hansard* printed by order of the legislature. Its contents differ considerably from today's publication. The speeches were somewhat condensed and reported in the third person, rather than verbatim, as they are now. Material delivered in French on the floor of the House was published in that language. A separate, unilingual French edition was printed by Roger, MacLean and Company.

Members of the Opposition made the most of the incident, comparing it to the spectacular scandal involving the construction of the Canadian Pacific Railway which had ended their own tenure in 1873. They eventually succeeded in forcing the Speaker's resignation.

The government tried to demonstrate that the irregularity had stopped as soon as it had been discovered. For example, stern memos from the Postmaster General, warning his subordinates to order all printing through the head office in Ottawa were produced in Parliament. But these warnings had not stopped the Post Office from making local purchases. Anglin's subcontractor had bought up a large supply of paper especially for the Post Office, and to help him work off this stock, the Department had continued ordering large quantities for many months after the disclosures were made. In 1877, partly as a result of this unfortunate incident, it became official government policy, for offices outside Ontario and Quebec, to purchase departmental printing and stationery in Ottawa, at contract rates.

But the efforts of Chamberlin and Young to supply these offices were not universally appreciated. The more the country felt the effects of the Queen's Printer's Act, the more loudly the printing and stationery trade howled in protest against centralized purchasing. *The Printer's Miscellany* charged that the government had taken from printers in Nova Scotia and New Brunswick "the chance to earn an honest living," and counselled subscribers to remember the issue during the next contest for seats in Parliament:

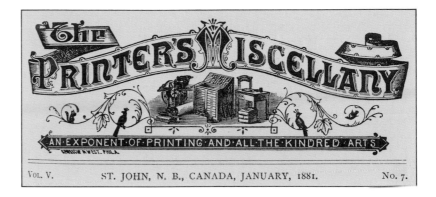

Ask them [the vote seekers] if they intend to take your money from you and spend it all at the capital for the very products you have in stock, and send them in small lots to the public departments right at your very door?

What was a politician to do? On the one hand, the public demanded fiscal reform; on the other, constituents made it plain that their vote depended on the doling out of patronage. And then, as now, there was hardly a constituency in the country without some kind of newspaper or job-printing office.

As we have seen, the problem resulted from a weakness in the Queen's Printer's Act itself. Section 7 of the Act allowed the government to employ printers other than the contractor for confidential work "from time to time." Thus, while the government was bound to uphold the official contractor's monopoly, it could at the same time still respond to the needs of the ravenous newspapers and print shops in the members' ridings. As early as 1870, only a year after the passing of the Act, the Joint Committee on the Printing of Parliament had warned:

Printing to a considerable amount has been done by different parties at prices largely in excess of the contract rates, some of this work being headed "confidential". . . . the law has been infringed by paying for printing, as confidential, at high prices when no Order in Council had been issued authorizing the same . . .

Politicians may have been prevented from feeding constituents with regular printing, but it was always possible to channel some "confidential" printing their way. And confidential work was not only awarded without tender (and without the orders in council called for under the Act), it was often paid for at much higher rates than ordinary printing under the contract.

This was justified on the grounds of the small press runs and extra precautions usually required for confidential work. But whether confidential or not, outside printing was often paid for at the high "confidential rates," which were suspiciously similar to those Desbarats had charged the government under the former patent system. In 1873, Queen's Printer Chamberlin was responsible for setting fixed confidential rates at 50 cents per 1,000 ems of composition and 50 cents per token of presswork— exactly what the government had paid George E. Desbarats for printing under the patent.

In 1877, the first year that departmental work outside Quebec and Ontario was ordered under the contract, Chamberlin reported that much less work had been given to firms other than to official contractors. That year, MacLean, Roger earned about $60,000 for printing at contract and confidential rates, whereas the value of work done by other firms, and audited by the Queen's Printer, dropped by more than 50 percent to less than $6,000. But only one year later Chamberlin warned: "There has been a considerable decrease . . . in the work performed by the Contractors during the year, with an increase of $62\frac{1}{2}$ p.c. in the work done by others." MacLean, Roger earned only about $46,000 for government printing in 1878, while the amount paid to other printers increased to over $9,000.

And what Chamberlin saw was only a small part of the problem. Each year, the *Public Accounts* showed large sums of money paid for printing over and above what appeared in the Queen's Printer's reports. Departments were still ordering printing no more confidential than immigration pamphlets and postal forms without obtaining Privy Council approval as required by the Queen's Printer's Act, and without submitting their accounts for audit to Chamberlin's office. Contrary to the intention of the law, the trickle of printing done outside the contract became a flood.

MacLean, Roger did not tolerate this loss of business for long. In January 1880, the company sued the Crown for breach of contract in the Exchequer Court. The petition cited breaches under both the parliamentary and the departmental contracts and included evidence taken from the *Public Accounts* to show that, from 1874 to 1879, over $225,000 worth of printing, which rightfully should have been MacLean, Roger's, had gone to other firms. Of this, the Queen's Printer had audited less than 20 percent.

Nevertheless, outside printing continued to increase year by year in proportion to the share of the work that went to MacLean, Roger. Having failed to stop the flow of work to local printers throughout the country, the government instead took steps to protect itself from further lawsuits. In 1879, the contracts for departmental printing, and for the printing of the *Statutes* and the *Canada Gazette*, had been awarded to G.P. Drummond, but MacLean, Roger, as subcontractor, continued to perform the work. In 1883, the Secretary of State recommended to the Privy Council that these contracts be transferred to the subcontractor in return for a guarantee that no further claims for lost profits would be entered against the government. The terms of this transaction, which were embodied in a formal agreement prepared by the Justice Department, were negotiated by Queen's Printer Chamberlin.

The following year, in 1884, the Court decided for MacLean, Roger in its first lawsuit. The Crown was ordered to pay the printing contractor almost $70,000 for lost profits. A subsequent judgment was also in the contractor's favour and the Crown had to pay interest on this sum.

In November 1884, the Privy Council approved a Treasury Board decision which stipulated that prices paid for printing outside the contract were to be kept in line with whatever rates were charged locally for similar kinds of work. While this ruling assumed that outside printers would continue to obtain government assignments, it did attempt to exert some control over the rates they could charge.

ADVERTISEMENTS.

THE OTTAWA TIMES
PRINTING AND PUBLISHING COMPANY,

OFFICE:

38 Sparks St., Centre Town.

THE OTTAWA DAILY TIMES,
Published every morning, (Sundays excepted,) at Six Dollars per annum.

THE OTTAWA WEEKLY TIMES,
Published every Friday, in time for the morning mail, at $1.00 per annum, paid in advance, or $1.50 if paid during the year.

The usual encouragement (ONE FREE COPY IN TEN) will be given to parties getting up clubs, whether for the DAILY or WEEKLY.

Letters, prepaid, and if containing Money REGISTERED, (in which case they will be at the risk of the undersigned) may be addressed,
PUBLISHER "TIMES," OTTAWA, ONTARIO.

JOB PRINTING,
FROM THE SMALLEST CARD TO A MAMMOTH POSTER,
Executed in the Neatest Style of the Art,
AND AT THE LOWEST PRICES.

THE EVENING MAIL PRINTED AT THE TIMES OFFICE,

The Ottawa Times **was published by MacLean, Roger and Company, the firm which obtained the parliamentary and departmental printing contracts in 1874.**

Your Committee are of opinion that if the Government, at an early day, had attached a Printing Office and Bindery to the Legislative Departments, many of the evils and extravagances which have grown upon the country, and a very large proportion of the money cost would have been saved.

**The Joint Committee on Printing
of both Houses,**
in a report to Parliament, 1859

he five-year contracts awarded in 1879 for printing, binding and paper for Parliament and the departments were to spell the end of the contract system. Already in serious trouble, the system probably suffered its greatest loss of credibility with the spectacular revelation that a scandalous bid-rigging scheme plagued the parliamentary printing arrangements. The scandal did not directly involve the Queen's Printer. It did, nevertheless, cast doubt on the integrity of the entire system of tendering for government printing, regardless of whether it was administered by the Joint Committee on Printing or by the Queen's Printer. More than any other single event, this scandal lent credence to the idea that the government should open its own printing establishment.

In November 1879, a series of articles in *The Globe* in Toronto charged that Patrick Boyle, proprietor of a competing newspaper, *The Irish Canadian*, was one of a group of printers involved in price fixing of parliamentary printing tenders earlier that year. *The Globe* claimed that Boyle had deliberately submitted, and then withdrawn, a bogus tender for the sole purpose of exacting financial compensation from MacLean, Roger whose bid, though higher, was eventually successful. Boyle published a series of letters of denial and, in an effort to salvage his good name, also charged *The Globe* with libel in the Court of Queen's Bench. Although testimony in court did not clarify the nature of Boyle's involvement, it did unearth a series of extraordinary business dealings.
It became quite clear

to the entire country that MacLean, Roger had obtained their parliamentary printing contract by "irregular and improper means."

Of the nine tenders offered for parliamentary printing, MacLean, Roger's successful bid had been sixth highest. The lowest bidder was Charles Henry Mackintosh, Mayor of Ottawa and proprietor of *The Ottawa Citizen*. However, Mackintosh and all the other bidders below MacLean, Roger (including the plaintiff Patrick Boyle) withdrew their tenders before the contract was awarded, and MacLean, Roger became the successful bidder.

The trial proceedings revealed that MacLean, Roger, or agents of the company, had controlled or bought off all the lower bids. First, the firm had formed a partnership with Mackintosh and submitted a low tender, quoting about $27,000 annually, over five years, in Mackintosh's name. MacLean, Roger's own tender was worth $34,000, but Roger testified that, if necessary, the partners would have taken on the work as a subcontract at the Mackintosh price. However, this expedient proved to be unnecessary, because the company had audaciously brought other weapons to bear.

VOL. XIII.—No. 11.   TORONTO, ONT., WEDNESDAY, MARCH 17, 1875.   PRICE 5 CENTS.

John Charles Roger had asked Edward John Charlton, a Montreal businessman, to submit yet another bid. Charlton's bid came in about halfway between that of Mackintosh and that of MacLean, Roger, and was used to pressure other low bidders. James Hope, who ran a small job-printing office in Ottawa, accepted $1,450 from MacLean, Roger's agent, Charlton, to withdraw his tender. Mackintosh in turn paid an unemployed printer, John Charles Boyce, $100 to sign yet another tender which, in reality, was submitted and controlled by Mackintosh. Having disposed of James Hope and John Charles Boyce, the combine had only Patrick Boyle's tender to contend with. Boyle's bid was about $1,000 below that of MacLean, Roger.

According to witnesses, Roger and Charlton had met Boyle in Ottawa to offer him money to withdraw his tender. But Boyle, who wondered why Roger was offering to pay him to withdraw when there were so many bids below his own, refused. Instead, Boyle suggested that, were he to become the successful bidder, he would share the contract with Roger. Then, claiming that he had never done anything crooked in his life and was too old to start, Boyle left the meeting abruptly, with a parting comment which was later widely quoted: "Yees might do it as yees liked." Charlton and Roger assumed Boyle was "putting on the pious," and meant that he did not want these machinations to be linked directly with his name. Since James Cotton, a close friend of Boyle's who happened to be staying as a guest in Roger's house, was also present at the meeting, Roger and Charlton

reasoned that Cotton had been empowered to handle the negotiations as Boyle's agent. Roger authorized Charlton to negotiate on his behalf and to pay Cotton up to $3,000 for the withdrawal of Boyle's tender.

A day or two later, Cotton arrived at Roger's home with Boyle's letter of withdrawal addressed to Henry Hartney, Clerk of the Joint Committee on Printing. For the letter, he collected the $3,000 in cash and some promissory notes. Roger and Charlton assumed that Cotton had collected this money on behalf of Boyle and that he would turn it over to him in return for withdrawing the tender. Roger, who was under the impression that he had paid $3,000 to eliminate Boyle from the bidding, was so pleased by Cotton's handling of the negotiations that he bought him a $24 suit—the sum of $24 represented more than two weeks' pay for a compositor.

But when the case came to trial, Boyle claimed he had received no bribe money. James Cotton testified that he had never worked as Boyle's agent, but rather in the interests of MacLean, Roger. Cotton had deposited the $3,000 to the credit of an Ottawa alderman, Michael Starrs, and had been using the money himself. He said that he had given Starrs the promissory notes as security for tenders and that the two men often bid for work together.

Starrs' testimony supported Cotton and Boyle's story. The letter of withdrawal, Starrs said, had fallen into Cotton's hands merely by chance: just as Boyle, who was visiting Starrs in Ottawa was writing his letter of withdrawal, Cotton stopped by. Boyle later claimed he had withdrawn simply because he thought

Mackintosh's lower tender would be accepted; he was anxious to get his $500 back and to return to Toronto. Cotton, seeing Boyle's letter, offered to drop it off at Parliament Hill; on the way, he had shown the letter to Roger and collected the fee. According to Starrs, Cotton had taken advantage of this simple misunderstanding to defraud MacLean, Roger of $3,000.

It was a good story, but it had a hitch. Starrs, with whom Cotton had deposited his money, was the Ottawa agent for Boyle's newspaper. Under questioning, Starrs admitted that he was in the practice of sending Boyle large, undisclosed sums of money for subscriptions to *The Irish Canadian*. Whether part of the $3,000 bribe went to Boyle via Starrs' subscription fees, or whether Cotton had really obtained the money under false pretenses from John Charles Roger, could not be determined. In either case, MacLean, Roger had paid $1,450 to Hope and $3,000 to Cotton for Boyle's withdrawal. On top of that, after the firm signed its contract, Mayor Mackintosh demanded another hefty $12,000 for his part in the proceedings. Thus, MacLean, Roger was poorer by nearly $16,500 and a suit of clothes. Newspapers speculated that the price which Parliament paid for printing was inflated by at least this amount.

In his charge to the jury, the judge expressed a hope that some public good would result from the incident: that Parliament would finally take action to reform the existing tendering process.

The Joint Committee on Printing had no choice but to launch its own investigation, which gave MacLean, Roger a chance to present its side of the story. The successful tender, though sixth highest, was still lower than any previous tender since 1868, and, the firm claimed, no one could possibly have done the work for less. The $16,500 "purchase price" would come off an allowance made for interest payments, and for wear and tear on the printing plant. Still, the company did admit that it would have done the work at Mackintosh's prices if necessary. And Patrick Boyle blustered that he would have been happy to carry out the work at his own, lower prices, which would have earned him a profit of $50,000 "without any trouble."

The investigating subcommittee showed more sympathy toward MacLean, Roger than toward the other bidders, whom they called blackmailers and extorters. There were even unpleasant insinuations that some of the members of the Joint Committee on Printing had known (and turned a blind eye towards) what was going on and had delayed their report to Parliament for several days to give MacLean, Roger time to get the competition out of the way. But since it was apparently common knowledge that buying off bogus tenders was a well-established practice of the time, there would have been nothing unusual about the committee members knowing about it too.

Besides, there was good reason for sympathy with MacLean, Roger. The fact that the contractor had an expensive printing plant, placed the firm in a weak position with respect to other bidders, who had

94

nothing to lose. Without the parliamentary printing contract, MacLean, Roger would have been forced to sell its plant to the successful bidder at less than half the actual value. This was so well-known that irresponsible tenders were submitted solely to take advantage of MacLean, Roger's vulnerability. According to Alexander MacLean:

... if they got the contract, we would be left with our plant on our hands. It was to avoid that, that we made the effort we did. We could not afford to run the risk of letting any other person take the contract if we could help it.

James Hope, the contractor who had been bought off for $1,450, testified that he had received money once before under similar circumstances. In 1874, Hope had been among those who had tendered for the parliamentary binding, but the contract had gone to Grisson, Frechette and Company at very low rates. Within a year, Grisson, Frechette were three months behind in their work, so Hope, whose bid had been the second lowest, was offered the contract. Instead of accepting the work at his own rates, Hope went to Alexander Mortimer, whose tender was third in line, and collected $500 for stepping out of the way.

MacLean, Roger also admitted to having obtained the 1874 parliamentary printing contract with the help of a bogus tender under the firm's control. And in 1880, as the investigation took place, MacLean, Roger was producing the departmental printing under a subcontract to G.P. Drummond, who had been awarded the contract as a result of an extremely low bid. Because this arrangement was under the jurisdiction of the Queen's Printer, questions about it were outside the terms of reference of the parliamentary investigation, but the circumstances seemed to point to another set of pay-offs designed to circumvent the intent of the contract system.

Faced with all of this, the Committee recommended that MacLean, Roger's contract be cancelled, and to "prevent in future the evils complained of," the Committee made a far more important recommendation: "that Parliament should perform its own printing."

Because MacLean, Roger had the only plant capable of performing the government's work in Ottawa, however, Parliament was in a sense a captive of the contractor. Cancellation would have to wait at least until after completion of the work of the current session. Several motions raised in Parliament to cancel MacLean, Roger's contract were never acted upon. Furthermore, because of the Committee's more important recommendation that Parliament perform its own printing, there would have been little justification for encouraging yet another printing contractor to open a large Ottawa establishment. Consequently, MacLean, Roger completed the term of the parliamentary contract. Moreover, by extensions to the firm's contracts, both the departmental and parliamentary printing continued to be done in MacLean, Roger's establishment for nearly a decade—until the proposed government establishment was finally ready.

*. . . I cannot see my way clear to recommend the
establishment of a government printing office on
the ground of economy,—as likely in fact to
secure the production of the work for less money
than is now paid.*

*But, on the other hand to procure such work
as would be creditable to the government and
the country, and greater facilities for its speedy
execution are objects so much to be desired as to
incline me to the opinion that it would be well
that the additional expense should be incurred.*

Brown Chamberlin,
Queen's Printer and Controller
of Stationery, 1885

n the spring of 1884, the

Joint Committee on Printing

renewed its recommendation that a government

printing facility be established. The Stationery

Office and Parliament had already ventured

into a form of competition with private

business by becoming their own importers

of stationery, a transition easily and success-

fully accomplished. Being seen to compete with

trade interests which were represented mostly

by importers of papers and other products

manufactured abroad was one thing; setting up a large printing operation run by government was quite another. It would be a risky, expensive, highly controversial step and, once taken, would be almost irreversible. Before venturing further, Brown Chamberlin, the Queen's Printer, was asked to conduct an inquiry.

Chamberlin obtained information from Britain, France and various other European countries about their government printing arrangements. He also travelled to Albany, Boston and Washington, D.C., where he acquired first-hand information about the printing operations of the American state and federal governments. At Prime Minister Macdonald's suggestion, the Queen's Printer was accompanied and assisted by Josiah Blackburn, a London, Ontario printer and publisher.

In January 1885, Chamberlin presented a report on the contemporary international government printing scene, which included a series of basic assumptions and recommendations that were to remain the philosophical cornerstone of Canadian government printing for the next 80 years.

Chamberlin's international survey supported his first recommendation, that the establishment of a government printing plant in Canada was advisable. According to Chamberlin, most government printing was done either under exclusive contracts with private firms or in government establishments administered by government officials. The practice by which Canadian departments procured much of their printing and stationery outside established contracts, on the open market, was nowhere recognized in theory, though in France, as in Canada, it had occurred in practice. All the government workshops Chamberlin studied seemed to have proven their worth. But wherever contracts for public printing and for paper supply were awarded on the basis of open competition, Chamberlin found that the contract system had proved as great a failure as it had in Canada.

In Boston, Chamberlin found that the same contractor had obtained the printing contract from the government of Massachusetts for 20 of the previous 25 years. As in Canada, the firm had managed to do this by tendering at prices not commensurate with good work and had resorted to indirect means of making the low rates pay. The contractor seemed to have no trouble making a large profit even though, on the face of it, the contract should have led to considerable loss, and the client complained of the same kinds of delays and inferior work that troubled the Canadian government.

In Albany, the New York State legislature had attempted to avoid such problems by awarding its printing contract at a lump sum. But here too, the contractors had developed an unacceptable means of turning a profit: the firm constantly endeavoured to execute as little work as possible. Suppliers went so far as to hold back work that came under the contract and to stimulate the passing of special resolutions in the legislature, requiring extra printing outside the terms of the contract, for which they could charge much higher prices.

In Great Britain, government printing and stationery were furnished by private firms under a variation of the contract system. Most of the suppliers had long held patents from the Crown, and their contracts, with relatively high prices, were not open to competition. Planned reforms were aimed at opening to tendering those contracts that were in the hands of former patent holders. Other work was distributed at fixed rates among private businesses selected, from time to time, by the departments. Because proper supervision and control would be so difficult under this option, Chamberlin ruled it out for Canada.

By contrast, Chamberlin could hardly restrain his excitement about what he saw in Washington, D.C., at the U.S. Government Printing Office: "No person who has taken an interest, as a man of business or one merely curious, in printing work as a great industry, can see it without a feeling of great gratification."

Chamberlin noted the office's cost-finding and job-tracking system—the use of a "jacket" or job bag, which would later be duplicated in Canada—and was pleased to learn that the method of tracking requisitions and deliveries of work was "almost precisely the same as that in use in my own office here."

The U.S. Government Printing Office had a plant worth over $600,000. A staff of over 2,000 people, paid at high wages, produced between $2.5 and $3.5 million worth of work annually. Such an enormous office was capable of producing work at great speeds; almost routinely performing production feats that would, in smaller print shops, be considered nothing short of miraculous.

Of course, Chamberlin noted that an office one tenth the size could never meet such expectations. He quoted the United States Public Printer's claim that "at times this office has had as high as twenty tons of long primer, brevier and nonpareil type, rule and figure work, locked up, awaiting return of proofs,—probably the largest amount of 'live matter' ever kept standing at one time in this or any other country." Chamberlin mused:

Yet for the report, in English and French, of the Commissioners for the Consolidation of our own statutes we shall have locked up from 4,800 to 5,000 pages of small pica and minion during the coming session. It will cost $15,000, and weigh about twenty-five tons. And it is not uncommon at the approach of a session to have a ton and a half of metal locked up in reports awaiting their revision and correction. Thus it will be seen that a very heavy strain may be put on the smaller office required to do our work.

Perhaps there was reason to believe that a Canadian government print shop might produce some smaller-scale miracles of its own.

Citing, as examples, other government-run print shops, Chamberlin recommended that the establishment of a Canadian public printing plant should not be justified primarily on the grounds of economy, but rather because of its importance to the public good. Chamberlin was particularly impressed by the French government's Imprimerie nationale, where work of high artistic or scientific merit, or work otherwise important to the nation, was produced at an additional expense precisely because it lacked immediate commercial value.

The Queen's Printer observed that government print shops in Paris, Vienna, Berlin and Washington had all been established for public convenience, efficiency and quality of work rather than on grounds of economy. That they produced better work with less delay was certain, but just how economically, was not clear.

On this point of economy, Chamberlin's views clearly contradicted those expressed by other advisors. Robert Romaine, long-time foreman under Desbarats and Derbishire, who was now Parliament's chief proofreader, insisted that, based on prices paid annually under the contract system, the whole cost of a government bureau could be recovered in five years.

Sterling P. Rounds, the United States Public Printer, claimed the U.S. Government Printing Office had saved the country 40 percent of the cost under

---

The High Cost of Printing at Low Contract Rates

Robert Romaine, Parliament's chief proofreader, was a former practical printer well-acquainted with the methods that printing contractors employed in composition to "blank" or space out matter by 20 to 40 percent, thereby making the low contract rates profitable:

Before the copy is sent down to the printer we examine it thoroughly, take out all duplicate and useless matter, condense and mark all head and date lines, signatures and addresses as close in as possible. But still all we can do and threaten [sic] we are often checkmated after we return our first galley proof, by several little dodges, as spacing out a few lines at the end of a few paragraphs in order to gain a few lines and thereby a page in making up a form. This blanking out practice in contract Government printing is a very old one . . .

The practices which Romaine described were more prevalent in departmental printing than they were in the parliamentary work. Because most of the departments had proofreaders with no experience in printing, they were unable to recognize unnecessary spacing and blanking out of material. As departmental printing increased, so did the contractor's opportunities to employ such ploys to increase profits.

Spacing out did not simply increase the amount of composition and the number of tokens of presswork to be paid. It also added to the quantity of paper purchased by the government; to the volumes of parliamentary papers to be bound, stored and shelved; and to the cost of shipping them around the Dominion.

To this, Romaine added the enormous cost of hauling printing paper, before and after printing, back and forth between Parliament's storage vaults and the printing contractor's establishment across the street; to the binders; back to Parliament again; and finally, to the departments for mailing. The same was true for the departmental contracts, which required the cartage of paper and printed matter between the Government Stationery Office, the contractors' establishments, the Queen's Printer's Branch and the client departments.

their former contract system. "I have no doubt," he assured the Joint Committee on Printing, "but that you would have the same experience should you establish a Government office."

Chamberlin, however, remained unconvinced. The Office in Washington charged at a rate that was higher than that charged under the contracts in the United States or in Canada, and the accounting method used by the government excluded the cost of rent and taxes, interest on capital or depreciation and renewal of the plant, all of which were financed and accounted for through different government agencies.

In fact, the Queen's Printer reported that he found it impossible to obtain figures that either proved or disproved the U.S. Public Printer's claim. Nor was it possible to prove or disprove the opposing view, widely held in Canada, "which might have been just a prejudice as well as a tradition," that anything done by government is always more expensive than that done by private industry.

Chamberlin recounted an incident which had occurred in France. A contractor had underbid the Imprimerie, which charged notoriously high rates, and had supposedly performed the legislative printing at a lower rate per page than the national workshop. On further examination, however, it was discovered that the contractor had shrewdly reduced the size of the page by a couple of thousand ems, and, paid as measured, was receiving more, not less, than the government's price. During this and numerous other investigations, the Imprimerie's claims had always been vindicated. But Chamberlin cautioned that the

evidence was no more conclusive about the relative costs of printing, either by the government or under contract, than the American figures were.

Chamberlin noted that if a government print shop were to be established for the public good in Canada, then the problem of delays, so common under the contract system, would be eliminated. Contractors had perfected a method of maintaining equipment and staff just large enough not to forfeit their contract, but not large enough to work really efficiently, and altogether insufficient for responding quickly to emergencies. Chamberlin believed that a public print shop, by contrast, should be maintained at a little above, rather than below, the absolute daily requirements. This was necessary to ensure that the relatively small Canadian printing plant would be able to meet not just the ordinary, but also the extraordinary requirements—to turn out great quantities of work in great haste—so essential to the smooth functioning of Parliament and the government departments. The requirement was doubly important in Ottawa, a small city without other large printing offices capable of helping during emergencies.

Chamberlin was unable to demonstrate that such a government print shop, dedicated to the public good, could be less costly than printing done under the contract system, in an establishment operated solely for profit. He did, however, identify a series of operating principles which, he suggested, were essential if the proposed government plant were to run economically and efficiently.

Most importantly, Chamberlin rejected the idea of a mixed system, whereby some portion of the government work would be purchased under contract. He reasoned that a government print shop dedicated to meeting Parliament's peak load demands, but unable to take on any outside, commercial work, would require every government job available to keep the presses running at other times, and to recoup the cost of this extraordinary service. In all the government establishments Chamberlin had studied, an absolute monopoly over government work was considered essential for an efficient operation, and every government job taken away from public print shops diminished their opportunities to economize.

Chamberlin translated a passage from a report to the Emperor Napoleon III, which reaffirmed this principle very strongly:

The Imperial Printing House, as at present organized is calculated to promote the perfecting of typography, and to assist intellectual progress by the gratuitous publication of works deserving such encouragement. . . . It produces typographic *chefs d'oeuvres*; it renders valuable services to letters and science, and it offers to the government for printing work guaranties of speed and secrecy, of correctness, and of superior excellence of execution, that would be sought in vain from private establishments. . . . And, even admitting the mere economy, it is certain that for printing which requires great despatch and special care, which requires to be done with the highest security for absolute secrecy and correctness, for which an immense establishment and a numerous body of employés is required there is no private establishment in a position to do what the Imperial Printing House does, not only at the same but even for a higher price.

To cover the expense of these special jobs, and of other printing such as the laws and court reports, government departments had to pay more for their work than the actual cost of composition, presswork and binding. As a result, the departments frequently defied the law by taking work to private printing offices, which charged lower rates. But this practice of distributing work among private establishments deprived the Imprimerie of the easy, profitable work, and drove its costs up even higher.

Moreover, Chamberlin learned that this was done not only because of the objectionably high tariff, but "also in consequence of the need felt to satisfy, to some extent, the claims of private industry."

Chamberlin judged that, if the government became its own printer, this tendency to distribute work to outside printers as patronage, which had already caused problems in Canada, could be "more dangerous to the experiment than anything else."

Patronage might even increase, not diminish, he

warned, if it resulted in the employment of unqualified management or staff at the government's printing plant. In order to operate efficiently, the shop and its various branches should be headed by practical people with proven ability in their fields.

Robert Romaine had already expressed his view that a practical printer acquainted with government and commercial printing should be at the head of the proposed bureau, someone not unlike himself:

. . . a printer who has served his five or six years apprenticeship to the business in all its details, one who as a boy has learned to wash an ink table and dry it from all moisture, and who can readily detect when a roller, after being washed and sponged, has lug enough to make good distribution; who when he becomes an older apprentice can put a job to press, make a good impression, who before he has completed his time will be well acquainted with book and job work. Such a printer, after he has travelled and worked as journeyman in other towns or cities, need not hesitate to start business on his own account, other things being equal. Such a Master Printer cannot be hood-winked or cheated by his foremen, journeymen and apprentices, as has often been the case with some of the printing contractors.

Chamberlin established the principle that the office should be headed by a businessman with at least ten years' experience as manager of a large printing or publishing establishment, though he did not go quite so far as Romaine in stressing the need for practical experience. "Actual training at the case and in the press room may not be absolutely necessary, though that would doubtless be of value."

Chamberlin's acceptance of the idea of establishing a government-run print shop was a cautious one. If patronage were avoided; if efficient management, a good staff and the best labour-saving devices were secured; and if all the government work were placed at its disposal, then, Chamberlin suggested, a government establishment might produce better work, with less delay, and perhaps even at the same price as had been produced under the contracts. Although his endorsement was qualified, it was, nevertheless, an endorsement.

. . . the rule of action in this case, the Government being the consumer, should be to get the best article at the least possible price.

Joseph Adolphe Chapleau,
Secretary of State,
speaking in the House of Commons on
Bill 132 respecting the Department of
Public Printing and Stationery, May 26, 1886

THE DEPARTMENT OF PUBLIC PRINTING AND STATIONERY

he government took a year to act on Chamberlin's recommendations. The Queen's Printer's report was in print early in 1885, but during that year's difficult session Parliament was primarily concerned with Louis Riel and the western uprisings. Besides, times were not auspicious for John A. Macdonald's Conservatives. In power since 1878, they had entered a period of decline. The ageing prime minister was failing rapidly, with no obvious successor, and growing regional interests and dissention within the Party itself were beginning to threaten his program of unity and nationalism. There also were claims from the Opposition that the proposed reform met some stiff resistance even from within Conservative Party ranks. Nevertheless, in the speech from the throne for 1886, the government promised to reform the system of government and parliamentary printing.

Secretary of State Joseph Adolphe Chapleau introduced the promised Bill 132 to establish a Department of Public Printing and Stationery on May 12, 1886, near the end of the session, which left little opportunity for lengthy discussion. The debate took place only a few days before Parliament prorogued, and just as the beleaguered Conservatives headed into another election. The Bill was passed on May 27, and "An Act respecting the Department of Public Printing and Stationery" became law on June 2, 1886.

By the terms of the Act, the Queen's Printer's Branch and the Stationery Office were reorganized into a new department with additional duties and wide-ranging powers. The Deputy Minister of this department, who was to report to Parliament through the Secretary of State, was to be called the Queen's Printer *and Controller of Stationery*. The Act also stipulated that the new department was to have centralized responsibility for all public printing, and was to purchase and supply all stationery required for Parliament and for government departments. Since the Department was also empowered to distribute and sell government books and publications, the Queen's Printer became, in a limited sense, the official publisher for Canada.

The organization and responsibilities of the Department, as set out in the statute, were based on international precedent and on Chamberlin's recommendations. As in most other countries, public printing was to be done in a government-owned print shop. Chamberlin had shown that elsewhere, such print shops operated less economically when some of the government's work was distributed to other firms. And in Great Britain, where government printing was divided among various print shops, the contractor who printed the British *Hansard* charged prices many times higher than the Canadian government was paying MacLean, Roger for similar work.

In Canada too, the contractor's extensive machinery and staff required for Parliament's printing could be maintained economically only by making enough departmental work available to keep the presses running between sessions. In fact, MacLean, Roger had demanded an extension to the departmental printing contract before agreeing to an extension of the parliamentary printing contract at the established rates. And when some of the departmental printing was given to other firms, the contractor had sued the Crown for lost profits. Consequently, Section 5 of the Act gave the government printing facility a monopoly over all government printing requirements:

A Government establishment shall be organized at Ottawa and shall be under the management of the Superintendent of Printing, in which establishment all printing, electrotyping, stereotyping, lithographing and binding and other work of like nature required for the service of the Parliament and Government of Canada shall be executed.

Such a monopoly was also expected to reform the well-established practice of distributing printing work in return for political favours. In its draft form, the Bill had retained the clause from the Queen's Printer's Act authorizing printing and binding to be done in commercial printing establishments in special cases. But the government soon gave in to Opposition demands that this offending section be struck out.

The Act imposed further conditions considered essential to the efficient operation of an industrial establishment. To ensure a businesslike operation, it was stipulated that the Department's chief officers were to be appointed on the basis of practical experience. The Queen's Printer had to have ten years' experience as manager of a Canadian printing establishment or as supervisor of government printing services. Qualifications for the Superintendent

of Printing, the Superintendent of Stationery and the Accountant were also defined by the legislation. The Superintendent of Printing was to hire and fire employees of the printing plant according to business requirements—the staff was not to consist of permanent employees subject to the provisions of the Civil Service Act.

The Act's provisions for the supply of stationery and printing paper followed a successful British model. In London an officer called the Controller of Stationery, at the helm of Her Majesty's Stationery Office, had long been responsible for all business connected with printing, binding or publication, and for supplying stationery to the public service. In 1882, the additional responsibility of providing these services to Parliament had also been placed under this officer's jurisdiction.

As had been done in Britain, the Public Printing and Stationery Act added the duties formerly carried out by Parliament's Stationery and Distribution Office to those functions already exercised by the Government Stationery Office. The Act authorized the Superintendent of Stationery to purchase and supply all printing paper and stationery required by government departments as well as by Parliament, and to distribute and sell all of their publications.

James Young's old stationery office had been so successful that the legislators who increased the establishment's responsibilities tried not to interfere with its former organization. Thus, early drafts of the Bill stipulated that stationery purchases should be approved by the Minister or the Queen's Printer, but

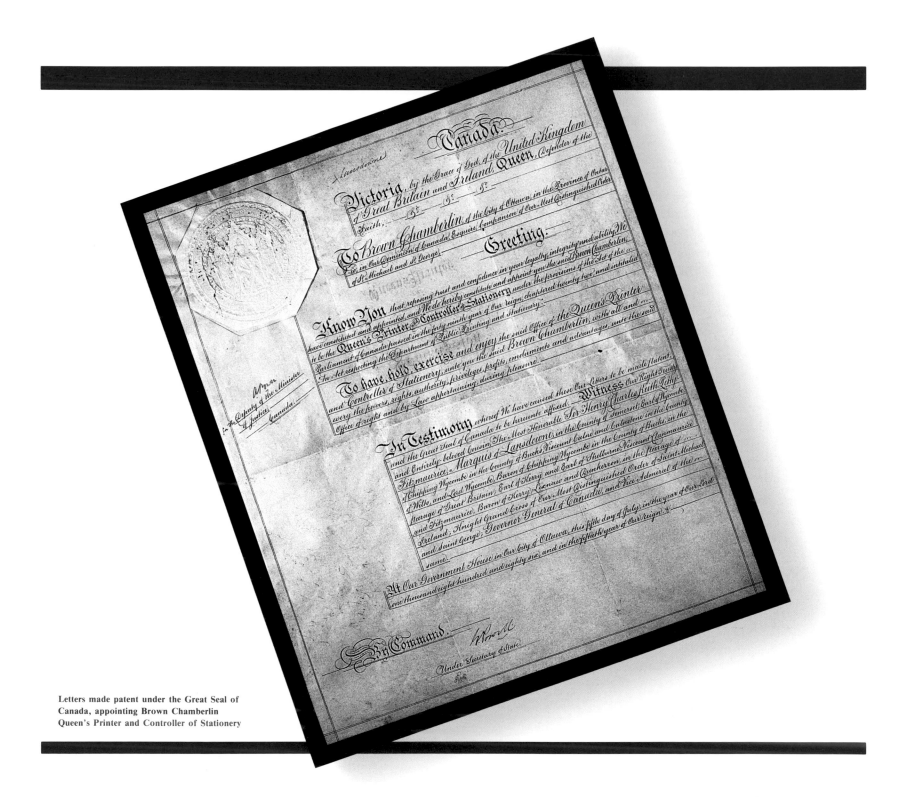

Letters made patent under the Great Seal of
Canada, appointing Brown Chamberlin
Queen's Printer and Controller of Stationery

did not establish any criteria for how those purchases should be made. Because of Opposition demands, the statute in its final version directed the Superintendent of Stationery to obtain at least a portion of his supplies—printing paper for Parliament, for the *Canada Gazette* and for departmental reports—on the basis of competitive tenders and contracts. He was still free to buy all other paper and stationery without tender, according to his best judgment.

Chamberlin had recommended earlier that the Act's most controversial element, the establishment of a government-operated printing facility, should not be justified mainly on economic grounds. However, an election was approaching and therefore it is not surprising that when Secretary of State Chapleau introduced the Bill he stressed reduced costs as its primary purpose: "the rule of action in this case, the Government being the consumer, should be to get the best article at the least possible price."

Chapleau declared that a government print shop would secure, besides economy, what he described as the necessities of government printing—"uniformity, quality, superiority of work, better security for the efficiency of the work, and secrecy"—but he stopped short of suggesting that any of these requirements, or that even some portion of the government printing, might be considered essential to the welfare of the nation.

Consequently, much of the ensuing debate addressed the contention that a government print shop was likely to save money. Opponents even quoted lengthy portions of Chamberlin's report that seemed to confirm their view. But the main objection was based on the traditional opposition to government involvement in any form of trading or manufacture. According to this view, even the prospect of potential savings could never justify what was considered an unwarranted infringement on the rights of private enterprise.

James Somerville (Brant North), one of the main opponents of the proposed printing bureau, described himself as a printer of 40 years' standing. Somerville ridiculed the government's proposal by describing how other industries might also be taken under its paternal care:

. . . why should not the printers of this country be protected from the Government taking up their trade in the way that is proposed by the hon. the Secretary of State? If the Government is desirous of saving money in this printing line, why do they not go into other branches of the service in the same way? . . . They have been paying exorbitant sums for cab-hire for the accommodation of Ministers and their deputies, and why not establish a livery stable, with a head and a deputy head, and a man as administrator, who understands horses and buggies, and a veterinary surgeon? Then if they are going to economize in this way, they might also establish a laundry and do their own washing . . .

Chapleau declared that his opponents represented "private interest against public interest, prejudice against progress, routine against reform." Both

Secretary of State Joseph Adolphe Chapleau resigned as Quebec's Premier to enter the federal cabinet in 1882. He was Secretary of State from then until 1891, and during those years was probably Quebec's most powerful and most popular Conservative politician.

Canada and Great Britain had established important exceptions to the general principle of opposing government involvement in manufacturing or trade. The government operated mail and telegraph services and had initiated the construction of important land and water transportation routes because these services were considered essential to the development of the nation. Opponents to the Bill claimed that they were speaking on behalf of the printing trades, yet even they did not suggest that there should be a return to the former system of separate tenders, which had proved so costly under the old Province of Canada. They argued that the existing contract system should be maintained. But, by this system, a monopoly had already been created whereby a single contractor claimed the right to perform all government printing. It would have made little difference to the nation's other printers if the establishment chosen to do all government printing were owned by a private contractor, as the Opposition demanded, or instead were owned by the government, as stipulated under the terms of the Public Printing and Stationery Act. The Bill passed and from that time onwards the government was established in the printing business. What sort of an impact this was to have on the country's other printers remained to be re-examined at a later date.

A Great Day for Brown Chamberlin

Early in July 1886, when the Public Printing and Stationery Act came into force, Brown Chamberlin became Queen's Printer and Controller of Stationery, and was appointed Deputy head of the new department. James Young, the Clerk in charge of the former stationery office, became the first superintendent of stationery, and 15 other employees were officially transferred from the Secretary of State to the Department of Public Printing and Stationery.

In honour of the new Queen's Printer and Controller of Stationery, all 45 employees of the Secretary of State Department attended a festive gathering, at which Under-Secretary of State Grant Powell presented Chamberlin with a handsomely inscribed copy of a congratulatory address. The presentation copy has not survived, but local newspapers enthusiastically reproduced its text in full. Chamberlin was touched by the testimonial, coming as it did from those with whom he had laboured for so many years, and who were consequently the best judges of his work. Among the presenters were the 15 clerks and messengers who were transferred, along with Brown Chamberlin and James Young, from the old

Brown Chamberlin, the Queen's Printer and Controller of Stationery. "The new position," he said, "will bring me more work, more worry, more responsibility, and I wish I could add to balance these, more pay." Chamberlin need not have worried about taking on a deputy minister's duties without additional pay. In 1888, an amendment to the Public Printing and Stationery Act eliminated the clause that initially limited him to his former salary of $2,400.

department to the new one.

From the Queen's Printer's Branch came Auguste Potvin, who had been in the office since George Edward Desbarats' time; Louis Armand Grison, hired in 1876 to audit the advertising accounts; George Andrews; Norbert Larochelle, who distributed the *Statutes*; Albert Olivier Mousseau; and William Gliddon, a practical printer and binder, who had been with the Branch since 1871, and who would soon become the Department's first accountant. From the Stationery Office Branch came an assistant stationery clerk, Thomas Robertson; Frank Slocum Gouldthrite, who had started as a messenger in 1879; William Walsh; and Thomas Roxborough, a future superintendent of stationery, who had been in the office since 1869. Four of the Secretary of State's seven messengers—John Hughes, Harry Allen, John Foran and Denis Beahan—also joined the new department, as did Charles Baskerville Sansom, a third class clerk from the Under-Secretary of State's office. This small group of men comprised the original staff of the Department of Public Printing and Stationery. However, it would be over three years before the new department would get the space and facilities it needed to carry out its mandate.

. . . a costly, magnificent, fine looking building, a monument of architecture, is not what is necessary. . . . we know that what is necessary for a good printing office is a large, well ventilated, well lighted, plain, brick building with a solid foundation on account of the heavy machinery and plant which is to be put there, and with just that neatness and simplicity which, while avoiding a large expenditure, will meet the requirements of such an establishment.

Joseph Adolphe Chapleau, Secretary of State, speaking in the House of Commons, May 26, 1886 he government allocated funds for the construction of the new printing establishment on the basis of Josiah Blackburn's rough estimates of the machinery and building that would be required. The Secretary of State expected construction to start immediately. However, in the first of several delays, detailed architectural plans for a suitable structure could not be drawn up because a site for

Prime Minister John A. Macdonald did not count himself among admirers of the Printing Bureau. "We were too poor at that time to put up an attractive building," he explained later. "One of the leading members of the Opposition alleged that we were bleeding the country 'white,' and in face of a charge like that we had to be content with the lowest expenditure on a building which would suit our purpose."

the project had not yet been determined.

Chapleau and Chamberlin wanted to build their printing bureau near Nepean Point, facing Major's Hill Park. This site was part of a large piece of land, directly across from Parliament Hill, on the Rideau Canal, and fronting the Ottawa River. The site had been reserved originally as Crown ordnance land. The government was fortunate to own such a large open space conveniently accessible to the parliamentary and departmental buildings on the Hill, to the Post Office and to the new Langevin building, or South Block, then under construction on Wellington Street. Located away from the developed parts of the city, the area would provide plenty of space for future expansion. It would also give the printers good natural light and afford the establishment some protection against fire from outside causes. Chapleau wrote to Prime Minister Macdonald:

If we could have permission to build there, ample room would be secured for the future as well as the present necessities of the establishment. Colonel Chamberlin will see you tomorrow for a few minutes if you have time to listen to him. I wish you could. I am sure he will bring you to our views on the subject.

Chamberlin did succeed, eventually, but only after the government's reluctance to commit itself to a location had delayed construction for a full year. This indecisiveness is puzzling, since the reserved land—Nepean Point and Major's Hill Park—had been considered a potential site for the print shop since at least

1884, when Robert Romaine pointed out its admirable qualities. The location's very desirability may have been the source of the difficulty. Situated on one of two prominent land points on either side of the Rideau Canal, Nepean Point afforded a spectacular view of the Ottawa River and Parliament Hill.

Once completed, the Printing Bureau was destined to come under attack from town planners and later governments who had more grandiose ideas for the site. Even in 1886, there likely were some who thought that a "costly, magnificent, fine looking . . . monument of architecture" would be more appropriate for the hill in plain view of Ottawa's Parliament Buildings, and who shuddered to think of the "large . . . plain, brick" factory Chapleau promised to build there.

When Parliament was dissolved in January of the following year, no progress had been made, and the project's future must have seemed uncertain. But the Conservatives were returned for another term, and on June 6, 1887, a construction contract was signed with local contractor John E. Askwith. Specifications still called for a building situated "upon the west side of the Rideau Canal in rear of the City Hall at Ottawa"; but when construction began, it was at Chapleau and Chamberlin's preferred location.

During the summer and fall, the building's foundation was nearly completed, and it seemed possible that the Department might be operating out of its own premises by the end of 1888. In anticipation of this opening date, a superintendent of printing was appointed. He was André Senécal, of Montreal, who was well-known among Canadian printers. Born in Boucherville, Senécal had served part of his apprenticeship to the printing trade with Chapleau's newspaper, *La Minerve*. He had gone on to manage several newspaper printing offices, but it was his most recent work at *L'Étendard*, a paper he was said to have saved from liquidation almost single-handedly, that had gained him a popular reputation as Quebec's finest printer.

Senécal needed several months to place orders for the requisite machinery and several more to put it all in place. He had spent 1887, and the early part of 1888, visiting major printing establishments in Canada and the United States, sometimes accompanied by Queen's Printer Chamberlin, who reported that their inspection of printing machinery in operation often yielded "very different results from those promised by catalogues and canvassers." Senécal made good use of the limited time available to him, ordering as often as possible from Canadian manufacturers or agents. The printing presses, however, were ordered directly from an American manufacturer, and much of the bindery equipment was imported from Great Britain.

Late in the spring of 1888, with $125,000 worth of machinery, type and other materials due to arrive in early October, Senécal was incensed to learn that not even a portion of the building would be ready for occupancy. He wrote:

The boilers and engines were delivered here at the end of September. . . . but the foundation for the engine has not yet been completed, nor is the floor of

N.° 7

SECTION on LINE A.B.

These renderings, which detail part of the Printing Bureau's front facade, and its main frame, were among drawings included with the contract documents to help clarify specifications for the proposed building.

116

the press room, or its heating apparatus, prepared to receive and place presses and set them to work.

Meanwhile, outside storage had to be found for much of the type and machinery as it arrived, creating additional expense and confusion. When the building was ready a year later, the presses were rusted and had to be cleaned before they could be installed.

The routine work of the Department was similarly hampered by the delays in construction. Without space and facilities the Queen's Printer was unable to fulfil his new mandate in all respects. He could not supply the parliamentary stationery, nor could he properly distribute and sell government publications. But in the summer of 1888, though still lacking its own facilities, the Department took over the parliamentary and departmental printing.

Ever since expiry of the contracts signed in 1879, printing, binding and printing paper had been procured under temporary arrangements made with the former contractors. By successive extensions, both the parliamentary and departmental printing contracts remained in the hands of MacLean, Roger. The departmental contract was due to expire on October 31, 1888, and the contract for parliamentary printing

on December 31, of the same year. With its new building delayed until May or June 1889, at the earliest, the Department was to be without its own printing facilities for another six or seven months; but MacLean, Roger refused to renew the contracts for less than a full year. Under these terms, the Queen's Printer feared that his costly new plant would remain idle from June until November 1889, and would then be only partly used until January 1890. Since no other printer in Ottawa could take up the work for such a short period of time, the Secretary of State recommended that the Department lease the contractors' establishment until its own printing plant was ready for operation. The contractor was paid $6,000 for a year's lease and another $10,000 as compensation for lost profits for the remaining months of the two contracts. On July 1, 1888, Senécal took possession of the leased premises. The binding, however, continued under extensions to the former contracts. Until the Printing Bureau became fully operational, Alex Mortimer's establishment, on Sparks Street, did the binding for Parliament and A.S. Woodburn, on Elgin Street, bound books for the departments. The printing, though done in the Wellington Street print shop, was at least under Senécal's supervision.

Although the building has been called plain and even heavy in outward appearance, it will not, I think, be possible to find anywhere one better suited for a printing office.

Samuel Edward Dawson,
Queen's Printer and Controller of Stationery,
1891

here are no records of the laying of a cornerstone or of any other ceremony to mark the Public Printing and Stationery Department's move to its own quarters. Only a brief note by André Senécal, the new Superintendent of Printing, documents October 15, 1889 as the date on which he set up the last piece of machinery in the new establishment and vacated the contractor's premises. Perhaps an industrial establishment was considered

The Printing Bureau, completed in 1889. When Samuel Edward Dawson became Queen's Printer and Controller of Stationery in 1891, he commented that ''although the building has been called plain and even heavy in outward appearance, it will not, I think, be possible to find anywhere one better suited for a printing office.''

The printing industry agreed. *The Inland Printer* ran an article about the establishment, which declared, ''the public printer at Washington, who has so often asked for the erection of a suitable building, and so far in vain, would feel envious if he took a tour through a building so well constructed and conveniently apportioned.''

unsuitable for official recognition. Almost certainly, the government feared that pomp and ceremony might bring more embarrassing publicity about the building's cost and plain appearance.

But despite contemporary opinion about its appearance, the new Printing Bureau was exactly what the Secretary of State had promised to build—a plain and functional structure. His goal of erecting a building perfectly suited to its function was admirably accomplished. A reporter from *The Evening Journal* in Ottawa who toured the establishment pronounced it "without doubt the best in North America," an opinion with which printing industry representatives unanimously agreed. Indeed, Canadian and American experts who visited the Printing Bureau described it as, if not the largest, at least the most complete and finest printing establishment in the world. At times, they were even moved to romantic excess. John Lovell, one of the most important Canadian printers of the time, declared:

I never in my life saw anything better laid out, and I have been in the best offices in London, England, in Edinburgh, Scotland, and in the United States, and I never saw anything to equal the Printing Bureau for order, system and anything pertaining to the arrangement of a Government Printing Bureau. I may say that I have had a great deal of experience. I know what Government work is,

and I know what is required. I say without hesitation that the establishment here is something grand.

Such effusive praise from printers was as common as complaints about the building's external appearance were from other quarters. But in the midst of all the controversy, Samuel Edward Dawson, Brown Chamberlin's successor as Queen's Printer, provided a balanced assessment. His description reveals what contemporaries might have expected of a printing establishment:

Everything about it has been planned with reference to the health and comfort of the work-people. Its detached situation and its park-like surroundings render it light, airy and salubrious to a degree most unusual for a printing office. It is substantial and strong, and, although enormous weights are carried upon every floor, no sign of settlement has appeared. Being built directly upon the limestone rock the foundation is firm and no tremor can be noticed when the whole of the machinery is in motion. Excepting the attic, where no work is done, the building is fire-proof.

That Dawson singled out the stability of the building for particular comment may seem surprising, but in Ottawa the issue was especially relevant. A few years earlier, the combined weight of standing type, imposing stones and printing presses had almost caused MacLean, Roger and Company's five-storey building to collapse. The contractor was able to save it by the hurried installation of extra support beams just when it seemed the structure was about to give way.

The Printing Bureau owed its extraordinary stability to the Department of Public Works design prepared in Chief Architect Thomas Fuller's office. The solid limestone foundation supported a three-storey red brick building, with a peaked roof and dormer windows. Above ground the foundation was faced with Nepean stone, which was also used as a dressing on the building's walls. Each floor was constructed of a system of iron joists and girders supported by iron columns and interspersed with brick vaulting. The corridors, stairways, engine and press-rooms had stone floors, and all interior dividing walls were of solid brick. Hoists and staircases built outside the building's main walls provided additional protection from fire. The attic, framed in wood, was more susceptible to fire, though the peaked roof was sheathed in galvanized iron.

The building was **E** shaped. Its front portion, which faced St. Patrick Street, was 207 feet long and 54 feet wide. Attached to this were two 70-foot-long end wings, which were also 54 feet wide. The smaller, central projection was only one storey high, and housed the plant's boiler room.

The power plant was installed by the Polson Iron Works Company of Toronto. Three boilers, two in use and one spare, were located in the basement, where there was also a storage area for wood fuel and for heavy papers. Every day, the boilers consumed up to two tons of wood to generate the steam required to heat the building and to run two steam engines providing 120 horsepower.

Today, this much power would suffice to run just the two web presses used to print *Hansard*; in 1889, it was enough to run the entire plant. The engines were on the ground floor near the building's front entrance. A system of overhead shafts and belts running from the engine room throughout the entire building connected the engines by pulleys and clutches to the various machines.

The rest of the ground floor's central area and its east wing were used for shipping and distribution offices and for flat paper storage. The entire west wing was occupied by an enormous pressroom. On the second floor, above the pressroom, was the parliamentary composition room. The central core at this level contained the offices of the superintendents, the chief accountant and others. The east wing provided more storage rooms for light stationery and small wares.

Two large binderies, one for pamphlets, the other for books, occupied a large portion of the third storey. An additional typesetting room located there was probably reserved for the preparation of forms, letterheads and similar jobs. Composition for the

Dominion's electoral lists had another room to itself because it required enormous quantities of type to be kept standing in galleys and readily accessible. The stereotyping room with its small furnace was also on the third storey, close to the attic where the stereoplates were stored.

According to all contemporary accounts, the plant had no surplus or inappropriate capabilities. A few years later, the new Queen's Printer, Samuel Edward Dawson, was surprised to find only one mistake in the selection of machinery. This was a small calendering machine, intended for glazing of cloth or paper, which remained unused. It must be added, however, that Senécal's machine shop also remained unused for years. Everything worked so well that it was far cheaper to have light repairs done outside than to take a machinist on staff. "Work could be done there with great economy," ventured John Lovell. "I do not think there is a bit of extravagance in that building as to order and system."

I have been in the best offices in London, England, in Edinburgh, Scotland, and in the United States, and I never saw anything to equal the Printing Bureau for order, system and anything pertaining to the arrangement of a Government Printing Bureau. . . . the establishment here is something grand.

John Lovell,
Master Printer and former parliamentary
printing contractor, 1891

More impressive than the Printing Bureau building itself was the equipment which André Senécal had selected. Each area of the plant was a testimonial to his careful study of the printing services required by Parliament and the departments, and of the latest improvements in printing technology. Senécal set up a printing plant that boasted "everything that modern ingenuity has contributed to the printer's trade." At the same time, he accomplished the

These compositors were photographed after 1891, when the Printing Bureau's first emergency power back-up system was installed. It consisted of 1,200 electric light bulbs, and an electric generator to power them. The new bulbs are clearly visible beside the original gas-lighting jets. Though electric lights were soon used on a regular basis, they were first installed because Superintendent of Printing, André Senécal, considered city gas too unreliable for compositors working at night. Any power interruption during the session could have interfered with the daily printing required for Parliament.

difficult but crucial task of acquiring only machinery perfectly adapted to actual requirements.

Composition

The Printing Bureau's presses were all power-driven, but the type from which they printed was still set entirely by hand. Unlike the printing press, the tools and methods employed by the hand compositor had not changed since the early days of printing in Canada, and the Bureau's composition rooms differed from those in earlier government printing offices mostly in their size. Working by hand, numerous compositors were required to keep up with the steam presses, and they accounted for about half the plant's regular staff at this time. During parliamentary sessions, and for special jobs, many more were employed temporarily. In 1889, when the Printing Bureau was near completion, Senécal engaged 40 extra compositors for the sessional work and 145 others to update the voters' lists.

Of course, this number of compositors used enormous quantities of type—the Printing Bureau had over 200,000 pounds of it in a great variety of sizes and styles. The type was purchased from several suppliers, including two type foundries then in business in Canada, which Senécal was directed to patronize equally. The oldest, Montreal's Dominion Type Foundry, furnished the greatest variety of fonts: nonpareil, minion, bourgeois, long primer, small pica and specialty fonts. A font of brevier came from J.T. Johnson's newly established Toronto Type Foundry, which afterwards also furnished additional sorts for many other fonts. The Superintendent also purchased more than 12,000 pounds of used type from MacLean, Roger.

Specialty types not manufactured in Canada, such as German script and type for the printing of music, came from Miller & Richards, a Scottish type foundry, and from McKeller, Smith, Jordan & Company in Philadelphia. The Scottish foundry also provided a font of minion for the voters' lists because the Printing Bureau required more type for this job than one Canadian foundry could furnish in a short period of time: 160,000 pounds of minion delivered at the rate of 15,000 pounds a month. This one order for the voters' lists was thought to be the world's largest single order for type ever placed.

The Pressroom

The pressroom, which was hailed as the finest of its kind on the continent, contained sixteen flatbed-cylinder presses and seven Gordon-style platen presses for printing small items such as calling cards, bill heads and envelopes.

The cylinder presses were custom built to Senécal's order by Charles Potter, Jr., a leading American press manufacturer, whose firm claimed that these were the finest his company had built so far. Of several cylinder press styles available at that time, Senécal selected two as particularly suited to government printing requirements. For the high-

"It is the grandest sight I ever saw, to see the presses in that room. I have seen them in the old country but not to the extent and with the order and system I saw there to-day. It is really beautiful."

John Lovell, testifying before the Committee on Public Accounts, 1891

The Printing Bureau pressroom was photographed by George McLaughlin in 1891. *At left*, is the battery of two-revolution flatbed-cylinder presses; *at right*, the Gordon platens. Behind them, and barely discernible, are several drum-cylinder presses. The belts were connected by overhead shafts and gears to the steam engine, which powered all the machinery in this room.

At the Heart of the Operation

Drum-type cylinder presses were based on an old construction principle. The impression cylinder's circumference was twice the length of the flatbed, allowing the bed to return with each revolution of the drum. After the sheet was printed, the cylinder continued its rotation, while the bed returned and passed under the ink rollers. Part of the cylinder was cut away to permit the bed to pass underneath on its return cycle.

The impression cylinder of the two-revolution press was much smaller in diameter than that of a drum-type cylinder press capable of printing the same size sheet. Being smaller, the cylinder made two revolutions during each printing cycle; after the impression was complete, it automatically lifted to make its second rotation out of contact with the flatbed. During this rotation, the bed also returned a second time so that the type form lying in the bed was inked twice, once on each stroke. Compared to the drum-cylinder press, the two-revolution press with its smaller cylinder was more stable, and the second return of the bed resulted in a more perfect distribution of the ink on the type form.

American printer George P. Gordon, who obtained a patent in 1850, called his press the "Franklin" because he claimed that Benjamin Franklin had given him the idea for the press in a dream. But many other manufacturers in the United States produced their own versions of the Gordon-style platen press. The printing units of these presses consisted of two plane surfaces, the press bed and the platen, which came in contact with one another after the form was inked and a sheet of paper had been placed on the tympan. Once the impression was made, the bed moved for passage of the ink rollers while the platen opened for delivery of the printed sheet.

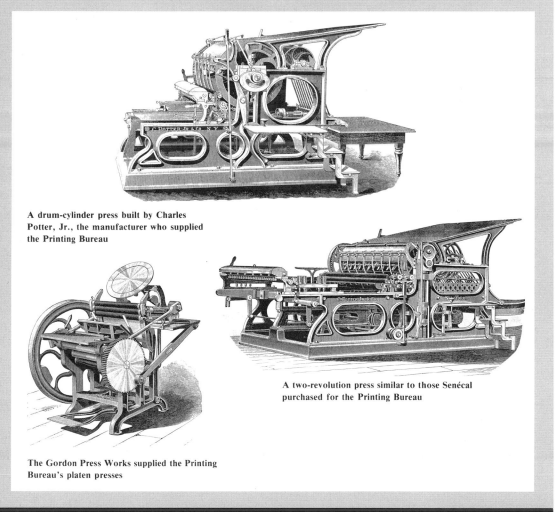

A drum-cylinder press built by Charles Potter, Jr., the manufacturer who supplied the Printing Bureau

A two-revolution press similar to those Senécal purchased for the Printing Bureau

The Gordon Press Works supplied the Printing Bureau's platen presses

129

It took two people—a pressman and a pressfeeder—to run the Printing Bureau's two-revolution cylinder presses. During long print runs, when there was no need to stop and change the type form, the presses could produce about 1,200 impressions per hour, but they averaged about 1,000. Pierre Desjardins, who recalls operating such presses at the Bureau, has described the difficulties of hand feeding the paper at such a pace on these machines. Each time a misfeed or other problem occurred, the feeder had to use a foot pedal to stop the cylinder before continuing.

quality printing of
parliamentary papers
and annual reports,
he installed ten large
two-revolution
cylinder presses.
These presses were
an improvement on the
older style single-
revolution, drum-type

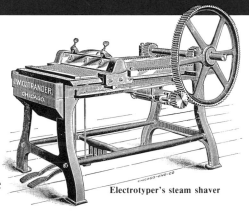

Electrotyper's steam shaver

cylinder press, and were used to print fine books and
illustrations. Two-revolution presses were capable of
printing long runs on very large sheets of paper.
Two of the Printing Bureau's largest presses printed
sheets measuring 40 x 50 inches. For other printing,
such as official forms and circulars, Senécal put in
six single-revolution cylinder presses, which were most
effective for printing smaller sheets in shorter runs.
They differed from the two-revolution presses in that
they had impression cylinders of a much larger
diameter, which made only one revolution during
each printing cycle. Four of the presses Senécal
installed were capable of printing on 25 x 35 inch
paper; the others, on somewhat smaller sheets.

The Bureau's platen presses were for printing
even smaller sheets, 9 x 13 and 10 x 15 inches. All
seven platen presses together cost much less than
even one of the two-revolution cylinder presses, thus
providing an inexpensive means of printing small-
format and short-run jobs. The sturdy little "Gordon
jobber" was a new kind of platen press which had
become extremely popular. It was easy to keep clean,
to make ready and to operate. The Gordons at the
Printing Bureau were steam-powered; one person
could easily operate such a "job" press manually by
using a foot treadle while feeding the sheets and
taking them out one by one.

Stereotyping Room

The Printing Bureau's presses were capable of
printing either from type forms or from printing
plates cast in metal by a process called stereotyping,
which produced a duplicate, or "stereotype," of
original type set by the compositor.

Stereotypes were manufactured in two stages.
First, the stereotyper made a papier-mâché mould of
the original type form. Then he filled the hardened
mould (also called a matrix) with molten metal,
which was usually an alloy of tin, lead and
antimony. After casting, the stereoplate was cut,
shaved and hand tooled. For use in a printing press,
it had to be mounted to the same height as the
original type. Several duplicate plates could be cast
from the same matrix, and these matrices as well as
the stereoplates could be stored for later use.

Stereotyping was hot, heavy and time-consuming
work, but the plates had many advantages and were
widely used. Stereotypes were less bulky and less
costly to store than locked-up type. They made it
possible to release original type for other purposes,
while preserving the work of compositors for later
reprinting without the sometimes prohibitive cost of
resetting the copy into type by hand.

Stereoplates had been used extensively by the contractors, but were first mentioned by Brown Chamberlin in 1885, when the first consolidation of the *Statutes* since Confederation was ready to go to press. Seeing that an earlier, pre-Confederation revision had long been out of print, the Queen's Printer arranged to have the new revision stereo-typed. From stereotype plates stored in the Printing Bureau's attic, repeated editions, or individual acts from the *The Revised Statutes* for 1886 could be printed as they were required. Duplicate plates were also used for shorter jobs requiring frequent reprints. Departmental forms or letterheads, bulletins or posters, could be reprinted from stereoplate many different times, while the compositors' work had to be done only once.

Stereoplates were perhaps even more important to the pressroom. All large jobs were routinely printed from stereotypes instead of type forms to reduce the type wear that occurred during long press runs. At the same time, stereoplates enhanced the effectiveness of the presses. If several duplicate plates were used on as many presses as desired, large editions requiring long press runs could be printed much more quickly.

The one drawback of stereoplates was that the metal used was relatively soft and wore down under extended use, thus reducing the sharpness of the printed word. More durable plates, called "electrotypes," were made of copper or nickel by a process using electricity. For jobs involving extremely hard wear on the press, or for illustrations and other material requiring fine precision printing, electrotype plates were either prepared at the Printing Bureau or purchased from other manufacturers.

The Bindery

The third-floor bindery boasted a fascinating variety of equipment, much of it manufactured in England. The many processes used in binding books—folding, sewing and stitching, cutting, gilding and blind tooling, embossing, finishing and ruling—required many more types of equipment than were used for printing them. Much of the machinery was steam powered, but bindery operations emphasized handwork and skilled craftsmanship. All the steps then used in bookbinding are still followed today, though the government now rarely requires skilled hand binding.

Bookbinding was carried out in two rooms, each with specialized functions. The smaller pamphlet bindery was equipped to produce leaflets, folders, magazines and paper-covered booklets. Here, large flat sheets which came off the presses were converted by folding into book sections, usually referred to as "signatures." For this job, Senécal provided eight steam-powered folding machines, six of them capable of folding signatures containing a large number of pages.

After they were folded, short pamphlets consisting of just one signature were ready to be fastened together into booklet form. Most publications, however, consisted of two or more sections which had to be assembled in proper sequence before they could be bound together.

Assembly work was all done manually and was extremely time-consuming. Most of it took place at a steam-powered revolving table, upon which the folded sections were placed in their proper sequence. Twelve women sat around the table, deftly gathering signatures as they whirled by and placing them one on top of the other to form blocks ready for fastening into book form.

For fastening, the establishment had a variety of thread-sewing and wire-stitching machinery. Wire-stitching machines, which used staples, made the least durable fastenings. The Bureau's five wire stitchers were used mostly for thin, paper-covered pamphlets and similar, inexpensive publications intended for relatively short-term use. More durable fastenings were produced on six thread-sewing machines.

Smyth thread-sewing machines, of which Senécal had four, sewed book sections together through their centrefolds and at the same time to one another. Other machines were used to sew signatures individually through their centres without connecting them together. This technique of sewing through the centre is called "saddle-sewing." Still used today, it produces very neat bindings. Even if they are bound into large volumes comprising numerous signatures, saddle-sewn sections result in books that open completely flat at any page.

Paper covers could be attached to the signatures during sewing or wire stitching, but publications which were to be hard-covered were always thread-sewn through the saddle. Hard covers, or "case" bindings, were manufactured in the other room, which was devoted to the production of case-bound books.

Hard-covered books were the result of a complex manufacturing process involving much skilled handwork as well as a number of highly specialized machines. Sometimes the same equipment was used for several different operations. The machines which cut the paper are a good example of this, because they were extremely important to a great variety of bindery work. Six guillotine-style paper cutters were used before or after printing to cut sheets, and before or after sewing to trim signatures. These machines also cut off the folded edges to free the pages and give the books a neat edge. Using a heavy knife that cut through a tightly clamped stack of paper, one side at a time, they were steam powered, with automatic blade and clamp action, and required an operator to position the paper for each cut. Six devices referred to as "press and plows" were used at the Printing Bureau to clamp books individually and trim them one at a time. There were so many cutters and trimmers at the Bureau that a knife-grinding machine was also required on the premises. Other cutting machinery was available in many different styles and sizes.

The sewn signatures had to be prepared before they were suitable for casing-in. The thread used in sewing caused the binding edges of the signatures to swell, creating an uneven quality. Before a book of signatures could be bound, it had to be compressed

A typical, nineteenth-century hand-gathering operation. The revolving table is steam powered.

A paper folder manufactured about 1882 by the Brown Folding Machine Company, which supplied the Printing Bureau. Most folders had a knife to make the first fold by forcing the centre of the sheet into a pair of rollers. Two operators, usually women, stood at each machine hand feeding the sheets and removing the completed signatures.

134

and brought to a uniform thickness. This process (which bookbinders refer to as "smashing") could be done by hand with a hammer, but was more easily accomplished with the help of a standing press or compressor. Senécal provided six large and three smaller standing presses and two hydraulic compressors. All were used as smashing presses, but like the paper cutters, they had other applications both before and after binding. For example, they could be used to flatten sheets as they came off the presses or to press freshly cased-in books until the adhesive which held book and case together dried.

Two additional shaping procedures, called "rounding" and "backing," were required to prepare signatures for casing-in. Rounding the binding edge of a book drew the entire book inward, resulting in the familiar half-moon shape of the book's fore edge. This protected the book by ensuring that it would remain inside its cover. During backing, the binding edge was creased and flattened, producing "joints," which provided the cover with the room necessary for opening and closing the book.

Rounding and backing could also be done with a hammer, but Senécal provided two hand-backing and two roller-backing machines. In the hand-backing machines, the book was pressed into a rounded shape, while the binder pounded its back to form the joints. In the roller-backing machines, the job was accomplished by a heavy roller which moved in an arc over the book, forcing its back outward and forming a joint.

Binder's press and plow

The cases themselves were manufactured and attached to the books almost entirely by hand. The bookbinder cut boards, cloth or leather coverings and lining materials to their proper sizes. A steam-powered case-smoothing machine was available for use on boards that were to be sheathed in cloth. But otherwise, the bookbinder used only hand tools to assemble and glue everything together, usually relying on a good eye to align material in perfect squares. Senécal installed three table shears with gauges to help ensure accuracy; a paring machine for leathers; and for the hard, thick boards, a powered rotary cutter and a sawing machine.

Decorations applied to book cases, edges and end papers were integral to the binding process, for they greatly enhanced the appearance of the finished book. Two edge treatments frequently used then at the Printing Bureau, but rarely seen today, were marbling and gilding. Marbling, which is no longer employed commercially, resulted in multicoloured, free-form patterns that could also be applied to the book's end sheets. Gilding was used to decorate one or more edges of a book; two gilding presses were used to clamp books under tension while their edges were burnished.

Two small presses—one for lettering and one for embossing—were used to stamp binder's cases with print and decorations. These presses could stamp with or without ink or foil and produce an image which was raised above or sunk below the surface of the case. Stamping that produced a raised image was called "embossing." If the image was indented, it was

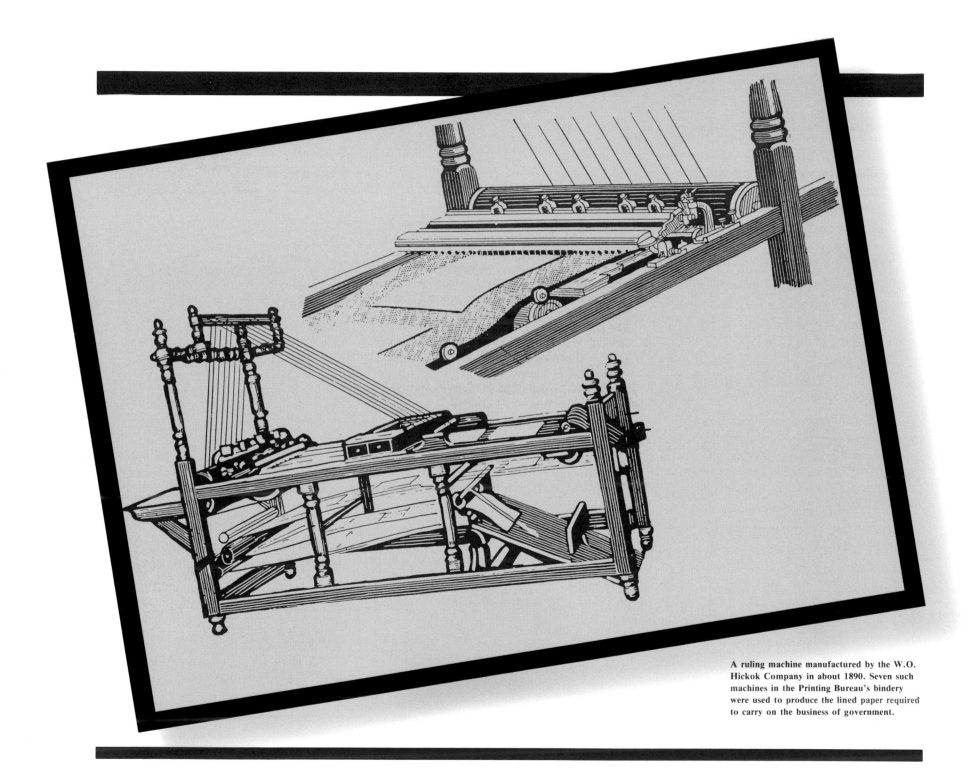

A ruling machine manufactured by the W.O. Hickok Company in about 1890. Seven such machines in the Printing Bureau's bindery were used to produce the lined paper required to carry on the business of government.

called "blind stamped." In addition, leather-covered cases could be finished with customized lettering and ornaments applied with a variety of hand-finishing tools, many of them designed and made by the binders themselves.

The bindery was also equipped to produce what were referred to as "account" or "blank" books. Since most government records were written in large bound books, such as ledgers and day books, this was an extremely important part of the work, which formerly had been done in specialized establishments.

At the Bureau, all the record books required by Parliament and the departments were made to order in the bindery. Ruling machines, of which the Printing Bureau had seven, were probably the most important blank-book equipment. They were used to rule sheets, which might also be printed with headings prior to binding. Seven paging and numbering machines were used to paginate the blank books. Other machines, such as eyelet hole punchers, index cutters and perforators, were used to produce forms, loose sheets, folders and bound volumes.

"Blank" books were sometimes very large, and could weigh as much as 50 pounds. Since record books often had to be handled daily, and were stored for many years, they had to be made with very durable materials and had to be bound together even more strongly than regular case-bound volumes. Sometimes printed or typewritten documents and pamphlets were indexed and bound in the same way as the blank books. Of course, chequebooks, note-books, diaries and similar items were produced in smaller formats, and numerous other stationery items, such as perforated forms, loose-leaf papers and folders, also required bindery work.

Printing

During the Bureau's first calendar year in operation, the compositors set nearly 45,000 pages in type, of which over 55,000 impressions were made in the pressroom. (One impression was counted as 250 printed copies of a sheet containing eight pages). This made over 13 million sheets which had to be folded and stitched in the pamphlet bindery. In the letterpress bindery, another 175,000 case-bound books were produced. Altogether, this work was worth about $160,000. Printing of the voters' lists was separately financed, and not included in these figures. These lists accounted for another 7,600 pages in type, of which about 2,000 impressions were made.

The variety and quantity of work turned out reflected, in part, the increased duties of the Queen's Printer under the Public Printing and Stationery Act. He had always been responsible for the *Statutes* and the *Canada Gazette*. Now, for the first time, he was responsible for the printing needed to ensure the smooth functioning of Parliament. This meant, in effect, that the requirements of Parliament became the Bureau's top priority.

Each session the departments' annual reports and other documents had to be ready for tabling in the House. These reports were usually published as pamphlets with blue paper covers and hence have long been referred to as "blue books." Ideally, the blue books were supposed to be completed during the parliamentary recess, so that their printing would not conflict with the heavy work of the session. In reality, however, this rarely happened. In 1890, Parliament

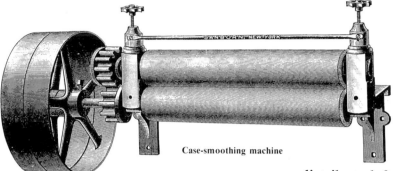

Case-smoothing machine

sat from January 16 to May 16, but Superintendent Senécal had received "printer's copy" for only half of the 24 annual reports by the first of December. Six more came in January, and the last three in February. Under such circumstances, Senécal refused to accept blame for any delays in the printing of those reports that had been submitted late. His frustration is understandable because, during the parliamentary session, daily printing frequently occupied most of the machinery and all the staff.

A night shift of extra compositors was required to set type in French and English for the *Votes and Proceedings*, the *Orders of the Day* and the Senate *Minutes*. These publications were printed early in the morning and delivered to the House by 10 a.m. The House of Commons *Hansard* was also begun during the night, but it was not delivered until the following afternoon, when the House assembled at 3 p.m. The daily *Hansard* was a bilingual publication, with speeches printed in the language in which they were delivered. The type was kept standing for several days, until translators completed their work and members of Parliament corrected their speeches. The

translated and corrected text for the revised English and French editions were likewise printed bit by bit daily, but several days after the first edition. Then, the type was distributed for further use. As long as pages were standing however, members enjoyed the privilege of ordering extra copies of their speeches. In 1890, some 90,000 copies of more than 1,000 pages of *Hansard* speeches were printed. The House of Commons and Senate *Journals*, parliamentary committee reports and legislation under consideration before Parliament were other sessional jobs that had to be done daily.

Responsibility for the authenticity and promulgation of the *Statutes* had long been associated with the Queen's Printer, who had also printed the bills (as drafts, for second and third reading) and in their final form (as acts) since before the time of Desbarats and Derbishire. At the Bureau, bills were printed daily in English and French as required. Printing the acts was also considered sessional work because laws had to be promulgated as soon after they received royal assent as possible. The *Statutes* were published in two volumes, with Volume II reserved for private legislation of interest to only a few individuals. A third collection of *Criminal Laws* was published for distribution to justices of the peace. Individual acts were also bound as pamphlets.

The other responsibility of the Queen's Printer was the *Canada Gazette*, which was still issued every Saturday morning. Chamberlin managed to sell approximately 70 subscriptions; the remaining 1,430 copies were distributed free of charge.

Another reason for the quantity and variety of the work turned out was the ever-increasing amount of printing ordered by government departments. Much of this was for business forms and stationery, blank books and similar items, but the departments were growing and were also issuing an increasing variety of publications besides their annual reports to Parliament. Departmental work was supposed to make economical use of the printing plant between sessions, but Senécal complained that, like the annual reports, half of this work was also ordered during the busy session of Parliament.

Senécal received letters of praise from many departments pleased by the improved service and by the quality of government publications. The regular night shift of compositors and the up-to-date equipment made needless delays and inconveniences a thing of the past. New type and much higher quality papers, manufactured in Canada and supplied by the Stationery Office, changed the appearance of publications almost overnight.

Universal rule shaper

Supplying Stationery and Distributing Government Publications

Of course, besides printing, the Department of Public Printing and Stationery produced other, less controversial work. Approximately half the building was devoted to the accounting and the stationery offices, and to the stationery storage areas. But unlike Senécal, who was able to begin printing in rented premises, the Superintendent of Stationery was hampered by lack of space and was unable to assume his expanded responsibilities until storage space became available in the new establishment.

In June 1888, James Young died, and the task of reorganizing the Stationery Office fell to his successor, Henry John Bronskill. This stationery expert was working for *The Gazette* in Montreal when Chapleau hired him. Originally from England, Bronskill had immigrated to Canada in 1872, and had at one time been attached to *The Ottawa Free Press*. During his first year as Superintendent, he increased Canadian purchases by about 38 percent. According to Bronskill, Canadian papers had improved greatly in the previous two or three years, and the papers he supplied for the printing for Parliament, the *Statutes* and the blue books were all made in Canada. Canadian paper was also much cheaper. Between 1889 and 1890, the cost of printing and binding did not change much, but as a result of the falling price of supplies Bronskill was able to cut the annual cost of printing paper from about $95,000 to $84,000. Interestingly enough, Senécal attributed

Officers and clerks of the Department of Public Printing and Stationery posed in front of the Printing Bureau for this photograph, taken in 1891. Not appearing in the picture are some 425 printing plant operatives, who were employed on an hourly basis, and were not considered part of the civil service staff. Queen's Printer Chamberlin is also absent, presumably because he preferred to operate out of his office in the East Block. *Left to right:* G. Baker, F. Thomas, P.L. Quinn, T. Flawn, G. Stroulger, J. Daly, G. Jessop, A. Baker, R. Niles, A. Riendeau, J. Gliddon, C.J. Peachy, I. Coté, A. Grison, A. Senécal, A. Hallaire, E. Carter, J. Byrne, J. Dufresne, W.J. McCoy, J. Auger, G. Hood, R. Edgar Cook, D. Pouliot, C. Wilson, J. Roy, W. McMahon, A. Filiatreault, J. McGillicuddy.

much of the improved look of government books to the higher quality of paper he was being supplied.

Another important innovation was Bronskill's introduction of a printed stock list. Considering the large quantities of stationery consumed, it is surprising that until 1889 departmental representatives had simply provided a general description of the articles they desired—a practice that resulted in what Bronskill called a "certain indefiniteness," with consequent waste of effort and materials. His printed list resulted in somewhat more specific orders, but "greater improvement could be effected," Bronskill noted, "if the list were taken as a guide in ordering."

In 1890, a Privy Council order sanctioned the new stock list and added new rules governing the supply of stationery to the departments. Items issued to the civil service through the Stationery Office were limited to those on the list. Embossed papers and other luxuries were either restricted to deputy ministers (and a few others) or were cancelled altogether. To obtain formerly popular items like dispatch boxes, brief bags and pocket knives, departments had to submit requisitions that were initialled by ministers, and showed the names and occupations of the intended users. Additions to the list could be made only by the Governor in Council. That year, Bronskill supplied some $176,000 worth of stationery and printing paper, and carried stock worth about $48,000.

Under Bronskill's superintendence, the Stationery Office maintained its prestige and expanded its reputation. Its most exciting development was the new Publications Office. As we have seen, prior to the passing of the Public Printing and Stationery Act, both Parliament and the departments engaged in large-scale free distribution of government publications. Often several copies of the same publication were sent from different offices to people whose names appeared on various distribution lists. Members of Parliament, senators and many others whose names were listed automatically received copies of everything printed, whether they wanted it or not. The only publications that were sold were the *Statutes* and the *Canada Gazette*, and this was only because under the former patent the Queen's Printer had enjoyed the right to profit from their sales.

This changed in 1886, when the Public Printing and Stationery Act gave the Queen's Printer and Controller of Stationery sole authority to sell and distribute government publications. Chamberlin pointed to the scandalous use of torn-up blue books and other government publications in the country's "hucksters' and butchers' shops," and hoped that a system of sales at cost prices might soon end profligate distribution practices.

But satisfactory methods of selling and distributing government publications were slow to evolve. As soon as the Act came into force, an Order in Council was passed fixing the prices to be charged for government publications. Following the British example, the public was to be charged only for the cost of paper and printing. The cost of composition was absorbed by the government because it was felt that this work had to be done in any case. Typesetting fees were to be charged only for special

Normand Larochelle, first chief of the
Publications Office, rendered 33 years of
faithful service, first with the Queen's
Printer's Branch, where he sold and
distributed the *Statutes*, and later with
the Department of Public Printing and
Stationery.

One of the Printing Bureau's offices

reports, and for those in such heavy demand that a second edition had to be prepared. Chamberlin's further recommendation, that one or more booksellers in each provincial capital and large city be authorized to sell government publications, was an idea that would not be accepted for many years. Nevertheless, prices were set at one-third above cost, so that a 25-percent discount could be allowed to those purchasing for resale. Under this system, a copy of the Printing Bureau's annual report could be bought for five cents.

Departments were asked to stop ordering extra reports to be printed, and were instructed to order only the number needed for Parliament and departmental use. Further distribution was handled by the Department of Public Printing and Stationery, where a few extra copies were also kept in stock for sale to the general public.

These functions were carried out from two separate Printing Bureau offices. The House of Commons Distribution Office, formerly located in the Parliament buildings, was moved to the Printing Bureau in 1890. Napoléon Boulet, who was in charge, was responsible for the free distribution of parliamentary papers according to distribution lists determined by the members. Sales of departmental reports, *Hansard* and the *Statutes* were all responsibilities of the Publications Office. Normand Larochelle, the Clerk in charge, had been responsible for the distribution and sale of the *Statutes* in the former Queen's Printer's Branch. Each year, the Office made steady, though painfully slow, progress in the number of publications sold. In 1890,

the Superintendent of Stationery proudly reported $152 worth of sales.

The following year, departmental publications were for the first time listed individually, by their titles. Such publications represented printing of half a million copies of some 11,000 pages. Their subject matter ranged from Exchequer and Supreme Court reports to rules for lightkeepers and budget speeches. A statistical yearbook, a census bulletin and reports on geological surveys, fisheries, minerals and other resources were important in a growing country. By far the largest producer of such publications was the Department of Agriculture, which was responsible not only for the widely distributed Experimental Farm bulletins and other agricultural publications, but also for ubiquitous immigration pamphlets with titles like "Yankee Agents" and "An Irish Farmer on the North-West."

Even at the nominal prices being charged, it would take many years before the public would get used to the idea of paying for material that they had been accustomed to receiving free of charge. It was not Chamberlin, but his successor, who first printed the prices of publications on their covers, and who published a list of government publications available for sale. In 1893, two years after Chamberlin's retirement, an Order in Council authorized the Secretary of State to place an advertisement announcing the sale of government publications in *Books and Notions*, a magazine devoted to the Canadian publishing industry.

. . . considering the past and present policy of the Government, with respect to their political patronage—there is great reason to fear that . . . the bureau will be a sort of political hospital and refuge for political favorites . . .

James Innes, M.P.,
speaking in the House of Commons,
May 26, 1886

he execution of printing in a government-run establishment was so controversial that during its early years the Department of Public Printing and Stationery remained under pressure to justify its existence. Though the vast improvements in appearance and timeliness of government publications were beyond dispute and immediately obvious even to the most casual observer, the thorny issue of public expenditure

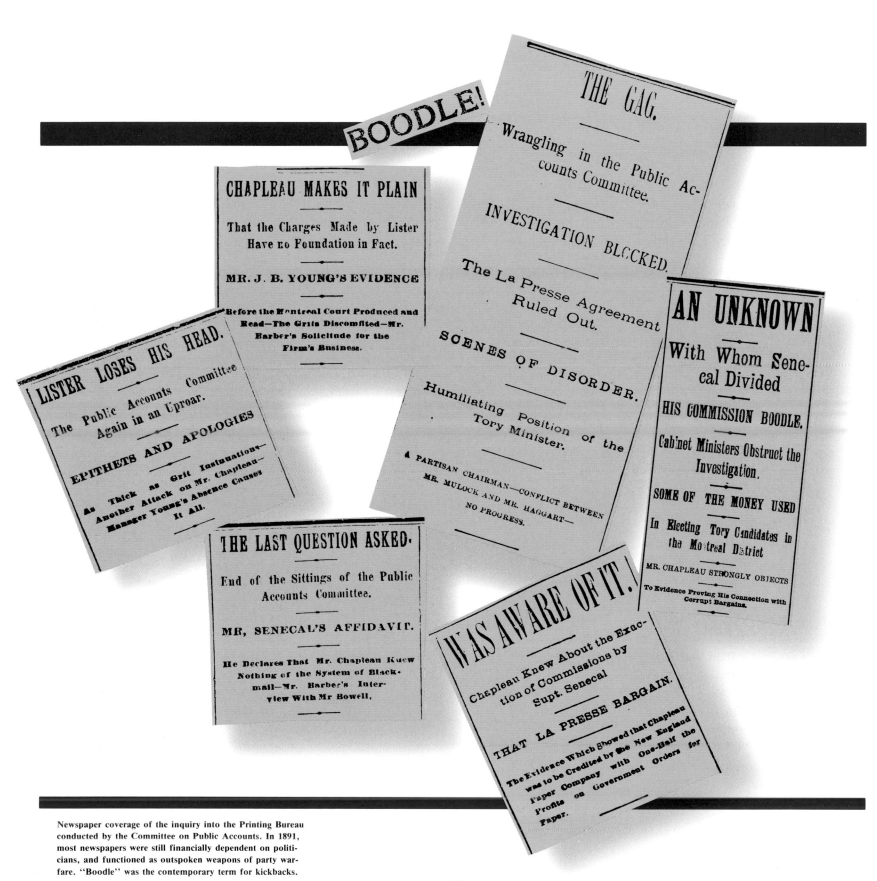

BOODLE!

THE GAG.

Wrangling in the Public Accounts Committee.

INVESTIGATION BLOCKED.

The La Presse Agreement Ruled Out.

SCENES OF DISORDER.

Humiliating Position of the Tory Minister.

A PARTISAN CHAIRMAN—CONFLICT BETWEEN MR. MULOCK AND MR. HAGGART— NO PROGRESS.

CHAPLEAU MAKES IT PLAIN

That the Charges Made by Lister Have no Foundation in Fact.

MR. J. B. YOUNG'S EVIDENCE

Before the Montreal Court Produced and Read—The Grits Discomfited—Mr. Barber's Solicitude for the Firm's Business.

LISTER LOSES HIS HEAD.

The Public Accounts Committee Again in an Uproar.

EPITHETS AND APOLOGIES

As Thick as Grit Insinuations— Another Attack on Mr. Chapleau— Manager Young's Absence Causes It All.

AN UNKNOWN

With Whom Senecal Divided

HIS COMMISSION BOODLE.

Cabinet Ministers Obstruct the Investigation.

SOME OF THE MONEY USED

In Electing Tory Candidates in the Montreal District

MR. CHAPLEAU STRONGLY OBJECTS

To Evidence Proving His Connection with Corrupt Bargains.

THE LAST QUESTION ASKED.

End of the Sittings of the Public Accounts Committee.

MR. SENECAL'S AFFIDAVIT.

He Declares That Mr. Chapleau Knew Nothing of the System of Black-mail—Mr. Barber's Inter-view With Mr Bowell.

WAS AWARE OF IT!

Chapleau Knew About the Exac-tion of Commissions by Supt. Senecal

THAT LA PRESSE BARGAIN.

The Evidence Which Showed that Chapleau was to be Credited by the New England Paper Company with One-Half the Profits on Government Orders for Paper.

Newspaper coverage of the inquiry into the Printing Bureau conducted by the Committee on Public Accounts. In 1891, most newspapers were still financially dependent on politi-cians, and functioned as outspoken weapons of party war-fare. ''Boodle'' was the contemporary term for kickbacks.

146

continued to haunt the Department.

In his report on government printing, Chamberlin had warned that the new system, which he supported, would not necessarily turn out to be less expensive than printing had been under the contract system. But the question of cost hounded him nevertheless, since the plant's efficiency and economy would not be demonstrated conclusively until several years after his retirement.

Between 1889 and 1890, prices fluctuated, and even increased, as a result of the confusion and extra work involved in a long-term reorganization. For example, departmental forms temporarily increased in price because many had to be reset from new type, so that new stereotype plates could be made. The contractors had been using old stereoplates that were either cast from partially worn type or were themselves badly worn. Prices continued to fluctuate as the new department tested and modified its first tentative methods for establishing the true costs of labour and materials and for charging these costs against client departments.

Under the former contracts, there had been almost no relationship between the actual cost of production and the prices charged for various jobs. Some prices were much below cost, while others represented an excessive profit margin. By the terms of their last contracts, MacLean, Roger had charged Parliament 25 cents for 1,000 ems of composition and the departments 10 cents for the same quantity. Evidence gathered by the Royal Commission on the Relations Between Capital and Labour showed that compositors' wages alone cost an average of 35 cents for that amount of work, but MacLean, Roger had more than covered their apparent losses—from profits on other work supplied under the departmental printing contract.

Each time a department ordered additional copies of a blank business form, the contractors charged for renewed composition, even though they could simply reprint the form from a stereoplate. They also charged the price of composition at least twice each time a table or column of figures appeared in a government publication—once for English, once for French—even though there were only minor alterations to be made in headings or titles. Many departmental reports consisted almost entirely of tabular matter, and identical tables frequently appeared in several publications, and reappeared with minor alterations, from year to year.

When the government or Parliament requested that matter be kept standing in type (to save the compositor's fee) MacLean, Roger charged five cents per 1,000 ems per month for storage. Under this system, the firm might well have collected a fee for keeping type standing under one contract, while charging for new composition of the same material each time copies were ordered under the other contract.

While prices were gradually revised to correspond to costs, departmental officers were understandably perplexed by new charges, which in some cases were decidedly higher than those charged by the contractors, and in others, considerably reduced. In general, the setting of plain, solid type, which constituted the bulk of the sessional work for Parliament, cost more after 1889 than it had under the contracts. As Chamberlin and Romaine had predicted, initial savings at the Bureau resulted almost entirely from departmental work. Once new stereotypes were made for the blank forms, departments no longer incurred composition charges when ordering copies of standard business forms or other repetitive material. Moreover, once the compositors were employed directly by Government, they were required to set new copy in an economical fashion, instead of spacing out the type to maximize the amount of composition and paper used at the press, as they had been encouraged to do under the former system. Even the reset blank forms reportedly saved the departments considerable sums of money.

In January 1890, nine months after assuming control of printing, Chamberlin announced a new, more satisfactory basis for charging the departments. He was confident enough to predict that the Printing Bureau would reduce costs by the end of the financial year, a claim which, for lack of conclusive statistics, had to remain mostly unsubstantiated. Chamberlin was able to offer only limited evidence to support his contention: during the Bureau's first nine months of operation in 1889, its largest departmental customer, the Post Office, spent just over $10,000 for printing, less than half the $21,700 this department had paid the contractor during a corresponding period in 1888.

Figures for the Bureau's first full fiscal year of operation (ending in 1890) confirmed that the Post Office had paid $15,700 compared to the $25,000 it had paid to the contractors during the previous year. These figures represented a financial saving of nearly 40 percent. However, the figures also showed that the Post Office was an exception, for there were more departments with increased expenditures than there were with reduced costs. Overall, the cost of printing for government departments decreased only slightly, from about $77,900 in 1889 to about $69,500 in 1890. During the same period, the charges for parliamentary printing, which had been executed by the contractor at a loss, increased by a startling 50 percent, from some $60,500 to about $91,800. Whereas between them Parliament and the departments had paid the contractors $138,382 in 1889, under the Department of Public Printing and Stationery their costs seemed to increase, for in 1890 they paid $161,418.

The figures alone simply could not substantiate Chamberlin's claim that printing had become cheaper. But because accounting procedures permitted no accurate comparisons between either the quantities or the cost of work turned out under the two systems, neither did the figures prove that printing had become more costly in the government-run establishment.

Though records of the quantity of printing produced by the contractors were not available, it is probable that rising printers' bills resulted not so much from higher costs as from the fact that more printing was being ordered. The business of government was growing rapidly, and printing requirements increased correspondingly each year. Perhaps the most striking example is that of the

Experimental Farm, which was instituted in 1886, at the same time as the Department of Public Printing and Stationery. Its first annual report, bearing the contractor's imprint, was a 58-page pamphlet. From that small beginning, the work of the Farm expanded so rapidly that within ten years its publications had increased, in number and size, until they almost equalled the reports of all the other departments combined. Additional printing for this department, which had never even been required of the contractors, nearly doubled departmental composition, presswork and binding at the Bureau.

In addition, the costs recorded for printing under the contracts had represented only a fraction of the government's real expenditure for printing before the Bureau was established: that portion ordered through the Queen's Printer. Sizeable sums spent outside the contracts for printing distributed as patronage were not included in the earlier figures. MacLean, Roger had proven in court, and been awarded damages, for lost profits on nearly one-quarter of a million dollars—representing work executed by other printers during a five-year period between 1879 and 1884. Such outside printing was now gradually being added to the Bureau's workload, further increasing the amount that was charged to the departments.

Under the contract system, the Queen's Printer and the Joint Committee on the Printing of Parliament had supplied contractors with printing paper. The cost of this paper had been recorded, but could not be used to estimate quantities of printing executed under each system. During the entire period the price

of paper had fluctuated; it decreased so rapidly between 1889 and 1890 that the cost of printing paper actually dropped, from approximately $95,000 to $84,000, despite the fact that the quantity of printing increased.

The most serious discrepancy between costs recorded for printing at the Bureau and for printing under the contracts resulted from the fact that Canadian government accounting methods suffered from the same shortcomings as those which Chamberlin had identified in the records of the U.S. Government Printing Office. Whereas the contractors' charges covered all costs related to the work – maintenance and renewal of the building and equipment, interest on loans, heat, light and other operating expenses—the Printing Bureau's charges against the departments covered only the cost of wages and materials and excluded all other items. As in all government departments, the Printing Bureau's expenses, other than labour and materials, were paid directly by parliamentary vote. When money was required for additional machinery or type, the

Secretary of State applied for the necessary funds through yearly estimates prepared for the consideration of Parliament. The House of Commons also voted funds to pay the salaries of the Department's officers and clerks and to meet the operating expenses of the Department of Public Works, which was

149

responsible for maintaining the Printing Bureau building.

Since all such costs were rendered under separate accounts, they remained invisible. And as Chamberlin had observed in his report, they made comparisons between the two systems almost meaningless and also prevented an accurate assessment of the real cost of printing in a government-run establishment. No matter how economically the Printing Bureau might operate, commercial printers could always charge that its so-called cost, reflecting expenses for labour and materials only, represented unfair competition with printers who had to charge prices to cover all their expenses and make a profit besides.

Chamberlin's report on the Bureau's first full year in operation was his last before retirement. When the report was released in January 1891, the reputation of his superintendent (and by extension, that of the whole establishment) was already suffering from early rumblings of what would soon erupt into a full-blown scandal. Though no hint of suspicion ever touched the Queen's Printer himself, Chamberlin was forced to spend the months before his November retirement watching the Select Standing Committee on Public Accounts investigate his new department and reading the opposition newspapers' gleeful daily reports referring to the Secretary of State as "Uncle Chapleau" and to the Department as the "Boodle Bureau."

In September 1890, the president of the Ottawa Conservative Association informed Prime Minister Macdonald of rumours that Printing Bureau suppliers had to bribe the Superintendent of Printing, André Senécal, with a ten percent "commission" for purchases that he made. The Queen's Printer confronted Senécal and warned him that the practice of accepting commissions, (which seems to have been widespread) made a civil servant a "dead man" officially. But Senécal scoffed at the accusation, and the matter might have been dropped had it not been for a series of political events which made inevitable a wide-ranging inquiry by the Committee on Public Accounts.

The Conservative Party managed to cling to power in the March 1891 general election, but when the Prime Minister died in June, the Party was in tatters. Scandal-mongering Liberals, and Conservatives fighting among themselves, caused one outrageous revelation after another. Public Works Minister Hector Louis Langevin, Chapleau's major rival in the Party, was perhaps the most spectacular casualty, and it was widely believed that the Secretary of State had helped to bring about his downfall. Now, with allegations of irregularities in the Printing Bureau, attention was focused on Chapleau, and opposition papers predicted that the Secretary of State, like the Minister of Public Works, would be ruined.

The most damning evidence against Chapleau came from a court case heard in Montreal in February 1891. The New England Paper Company, a paper manufacturer, had filed suit for breach of contract against the publisher of the Montreal newspaper, *La Presse*. The paper belonged to a company in which the Secretary of State was the major shareholder. After the trial, observers claimed that evidence had been presented, but subsequently struck from the record, which could have implicated the Secretary of State in a corrupt bargain.

When Chapleau's company had purchased *La Presse* from its former owners, the newspaper was indebted to the New England Paper Company for approximately $10,000. The newspaper's new editor, Trefflé Berthiaume, leased publishing rights from Chapleau's company and entered into an arrangement by which Berthiaume would assume the debt and the paper company would continue to supply him with printing paper.

Berthiaume and the New England Paper Company were parties to a contract which included a clause stating that the paper supplier would apply half of all the profits that the company earned on printing paper sales to the Department of Public Printing and Stationery towards interest due on the editor's loan. In court, the company president testified that he had agreed to the bargain on the understanding that his firm would receive government orders through the Secretary of State. He believed this partly because Joseph Adolphe Chapleau had endorsed Berthiaume's promissory notes.

The New England Paper Company had filed a lawsuit against *La Presse* because Berthiaume had suddenly paid off the promissory notes and, without giving notice, had abruptly terminated the printing paper-supply contract. He had borrowed the money from a rival paper manufacturer, from whom he subsequently purchased his newsprint. Oddly enough, the plaintiff's lawyer was a partner in Chapleau's law firm.

During the inquiry by the Committee on Public Accounts, Liberal minority members did their utmost to prove Chapleau's complicity. They did succeed in obtaining the text of the evidence missing from the court report, but failed to prove that the Secretary of State actually had been aware of the whole affair. The Printing Bureau had ordered only one shipment of printing paper from the New England Paper Company. Although the paper had turned out to be unsuitable, it was accepted at the Bureau by special request of the Secretary of State. Berthiaume, however, claimed afterwards that the paper company's profit from this transaction was so small that it had not been applied to the loan.

The Printing Bureau's superintendents were not as fortunate as the Secretary of State. One manufacturer after another testified that André Senécal had exacted "grease" money, sometimes extravagant sums, for his patronage. Early in the inquiry, the Superintendent was obliged to flee the country and what he called the Committee's "system of low spying and vile, anonymous informing." A letter Senécal left behind referred to the money he had received as "testimonials of esteem and of cordial relations from friend to friend," which he claimed had not interfered with his purchases, made at the lowest possible prices.

I have worked often—very often—late into the night to make the National Printing Office what it is, and my work will stand as my answer to the calumniators and fanatics who have sought my ruin.

The Committee's investigation revealed that Senécal had received cordial "testimonials" totalling about $50,000. But in the assessment of his work, at least, Senécal was vindicated. Manufacturers all corroborated that Senécal approached them for bribes only after prices had been negotiated. And the Department produced many witnesses, including important printers like John Lovell and former Queen's Printer George Edward Desbarats, who testified that they considered the establishment's equipment to be excellent, and the prices paid for it to be reasonable, or lower than they would have thought possible.

Stories of Senécal's machinations made a daily sensation in the press. Conservative newspaper accounts described the Superintendent as a vile and crafty criminal, while Liberal journals depicted him as an unfortunate victim, forced to collect "boodle" for the governing Conservatives and now offered up as a hapless scapegoat. A few weeks after the inquiry was over, Senécal returned to his Ottawa home, which, *The Ottawa Free Press* joked, did not look as if he

had invested $50,000 in it—thus implying the money had been used for political purposes. But, though Liberal members of the Committee tried hard, they failed to show a direct connection between Senécal's commissions and Conservative Party coffers.

Superintendent of Stationery Henry Bronskill also lost his job, all the while protesting his innocence. He admitted to having received a gift and a loan amounting to less than $200. While the circumstances actually did sound like a testimonial of esteem from a friend, Bronskill's unfortunate acceptance of this gift at this time led to his dismissal.

In the end, the inquiry produced evidence of wrongdoing on the part of only a few individuals, and the establishment underwent a minor reorganization. Until 1891, the superintendents and accountant had reported directly to the Secretary of State along with the Queen's Printer. From this time on, they would report to the Queen's Printer who would be responsible to the Secretary of State. The new clear line of command was supposed to prevent any future improprieties, but there were other problems, as yet unrecognized.

Even though the accusations against Chapleau were not proven, the nature of the questions surrounding paper purchases should have alerted the government to another serious flaw in the new department's organization. The Public Printing and Stationery Act still allowed the Superintendent of Stationery to make major purchases without tender, according to his own discretion and with the Minister's approval. As the departments continued

to grow, and as the Stationery Office expanded correspondingly, this provision of the Act became more and more inappropriate and later resulted in much more serious, even tragic, consequences.

For the time being, however, the Department recovered rapidly from the unpleasantness concerning the Committee on Public Accounts, though not before Chamberlin's retirement. It was left to Chamberlin's successor, Samuel Edward Dawson, outspoken publisher and stern administrator, to build the Printing Bureau into a highly respected operation.

The Public Printing and Stationery Act had originally required the Queen's Printer to have at least ten years' experience in the management of a printing establishment. In 1888, an amendment to the Act allowed the Queen's Printer to have gained the requisite experience either in publishing or in printing, thereby making Dawson, who was not a printer, eligible for the position.

The new Queen's Printer was a well-known author, publisher, bookseller and authority on various subjects, particularly international copyright. In 1890, when Laval University honoured him with the degree of doctor of letters, *The Dominion Illustrated* editorialized:

In learning that is by no means common—in constitutional knowledge, in the higher provinces of literary criticism, in thorough mastery of the principles of finance and commerce—he has no superior in Canada.

One of Dawson's first acts as Queen's Printer could be regarded as symbolic of his new regime: he

Samuel Edward Dawson

Born in Halifax on June 1, 1833, the young Samuel Edward moved with his family to Montreal. There he helped his father Benjamin establish a book and stationery business. Later, when his father left the business to become a minister, the store became Dawson Brothers, with Samuel Edward as the senior partner.

The bookshop enjoyed success and a good reputation, playing a prominent role in the Dominion's literary circles. Like other large booksellers, Dawson Brothers soon became book publishers, listing primarily legal, scientific and technical works. In 1880, Samuel Edward Dawson and an employee, E.N. Renouf, formed the Montreal News Company, which distributed books, magazines and newspapers throughout Quebec and the Maritime provinces. After Samuel Edward withdrew from the publishing business, Renouf took over the publishing side of Dawson Brothers and specialized in scientific books.

Meanwhile Samuel Edward himself became known for his writings on literature, geography and history. Much of his scholarly work appeared in the *Proceedings and Transactions* of the Royal Society of Canada, of which he was a founding member and later a president. Dawson was also a frequent contributor to other Canadian and foreign journals and newspapers. Among his important monographs were *A Study, With Critical and Explanatory Notes, of Lord Tennyson's Poem, "The Princess"* (published in 1882), *Handbook of the Dominion of Canada* (1884) and *The St. Lawrence Basin* (1905).

Samuel Edward Dawson
Queen's Printer and Controller of Stationery 1891 to 1909.
"I have a very strong opinion that six hours real work should be taken out of every man . . . and as soon as I can get my office moved to the Bureau, I shall enforce it."

Reviewers frequently noted Dawson's "strong patriotic feeling . . . and a certain bias in favour of things Canadian." Dawson did consider himself a spokesman for Canada, once describing one of his books as:

. . . a tribute to our Country's history. . . . I wrote it more for England than Canada. The English know so little about the country and its very remarkable history that I wrote the book almost as a duty.

As an author and book publisher, Dawson was vitally concerned with the development of Canadian copyright legislation. He became an expert on the subject, and his advocacy on behalf of Canadian authors and publishers was an important contribution to the development of a national publishing industry. In 1881 and 1882, he attended an international copyright conference in Washington as advisor to the Canadian delegate, Sir Leonard Tilley. Dawson's lecture to the Law Faculty of Bishop's College in Lennoxville, Quebec, entitled *Copyright in Books*, was widely quoted and published as a pamphlet in 1882.

Dawson retired from his career in commercial publishing to become the Queen's Printer at the age of 58. He brought to the Printing Bureau the same unflagging energy and meticulous attention to detail that characterized him as an author and publisher. On his 75th birthday, after he had reportedly served for 17 years without a day's sick leave, Dawson was forced by health problems to take an extended leave, and afterwards to retire. He died at his home in Montreal on February 10, 1916.

PRINTERS' PRIDE
OR BOODLE BUREAU
PRINTERS' PRIDE
OR BOODLE BUREAU

abolished the two-hour lunch break which in other departments still formed an accepted part of the civil servant's very civilized 9:30 a.m. to 4 p.m. routine. In order to supervise his staff more closely, Dawson moved from the East Block to the Printing Bureau, establishing himself in a large ground floor space close to the building's main entrance. From this roomy alcove, reportedly lined with bookshelves, he could keep a sharp eye on the operation. Dawson believed that close, daily contact with the staff promoted a "greater unity of effort." He devoted the same meticulous personal attention to every issue, great or small, and would be just as likely to initiate a sweeping organizational change as to dash off a stern memo rebuking the Under-Secretary of State for trying to requisition 35 pocket knives "not according to law."

Queen's Printer Dawson approached questions about the cost of printing at the Bureau with char-

acteristic energy. Immediately after his appointment in December 1891, only a few months after the inquiry by the Committee on Public Accounts, a royal commission conducting an investigation into the civil service visited the Printing Bureau and heard Dawson's testimony that his establishment was a highly efficient one. The commissioners concluded:

Great economies have been introduced in the management of the masses of printing and stationery required by the Government, and the erection of the building and the placing therein the improved machinery and quantity of type it contains has been amply justified by the result.

So effective was Dawson's presentation that the commissioners gave the new Queen's Printer particular credit for this economy, even though Dawson had been in office for little more than a month!

155

. . . if the government purchased those machines
they would be misusing the people's money and
besides Canadians would be driven abroad to
seek a livelihood.

The Ottawa Daily Free Press,
describing a resolution which the Ottawa
Typographical Union (Local 102) presented
to the Minister of Finance,
May 14, 1890

ueen's Printer Dawson can be credited with having built the new print shop into one of the world's finest government printing establishments. A few of his innovations are still integral to the printing organization as it exists today. The change that had the most direct impact on the staff, however, was his full implementation of mechanized composition. Typesetting machines had been introduced to the Bureau less than two years

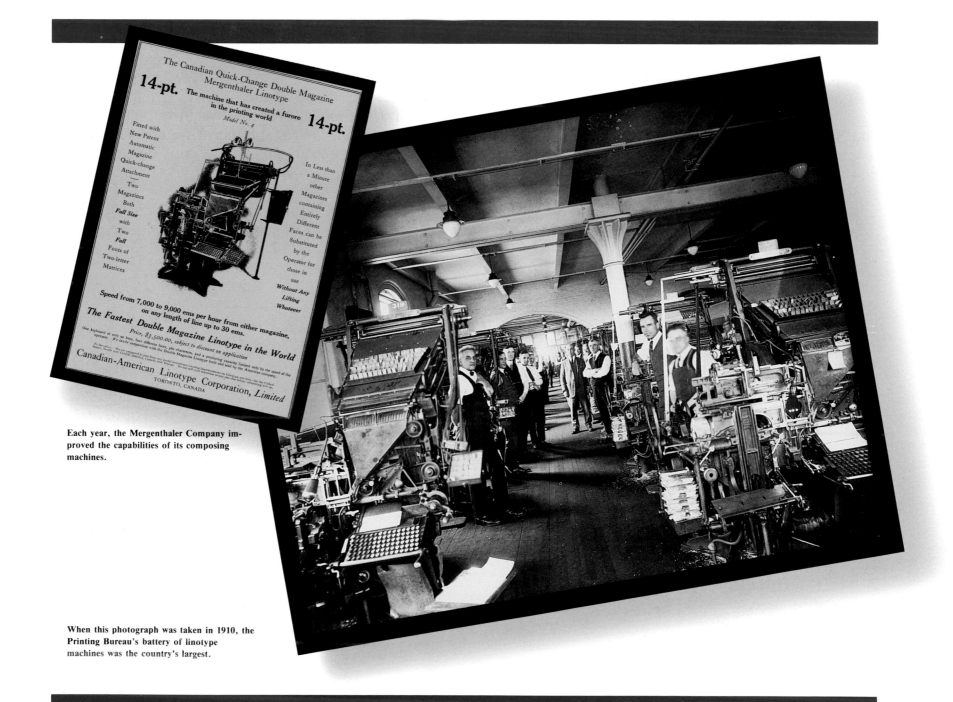

Each year, the Mergenthaler Company improved the capabilities of its composing machines.

When this photograph was taken in 1910, the Printing Bureau's battery of linotype machines was the country's largest.

after its establishment, and several months before Dawson's arrival.

In October 1890, Queen's Printer Chamberlin and Superintendent of Printing Senécal were on a scouting expedition in New York City in search of new printing technology. There, they were so impressed by improvements in the Mergenthaler Company's recently inaugurated linotype machines that they purchased four of the machines on the spot. Within four months, these linotypes were installed at the Bureau, and four operators had been trained to use them. For the first two months of the parliamentary session of 1891, until the end of June, the machines were used experimentally to set the Senate *Debates*.

The successful development of a machine that enabled typesetters to set type four or five times faster than was possible by hand created turmoil, not just at the Printing Bureau, but in printing offices everywhere. Whereas the processes of mechanizing the pressroom and bindery had been continual and diversified, the transition from hand to machine composition was a sudden, single change. Compositors facing mechanization for the first time feared they might become redundant because of the linotype. They worried about the possibility that they would not have the opportunity to learn the operation of the new machines, but would instead be replaced by less skilled, less costly labour. Compositors, like those at the Printing Bureau, feared the worst, but employers saw in the machines the long awaited opportunity to overcome the bottleneck that existed in the composing room.

Dawson claimed that the Printing Bureau was the first office in Canada to use typesetting machinery. Though *The Globe* in Toronto routinely claimed the same distinction, that establishment's union records do not mention typesetting machinery until December 1891. According to the *Printer and Publisher*, the first Canadian-built linotype machines were shipped from Montreal to the offices of *The Globe* on March 12, 1892, about a year after typesetting machines purchased from the manufacturer in New York were introduced at the Printing Bureau.

While Dawson did not introduce the machines himself, he was first to fully exploit the new technology. When he became Queen's Printer in November 1891, the widely disliked linotype machines had already fallen into disrepair and were no longer used. This annoyed Dawson, since typesetting by machine offered an ideal opportunity to reduce the cost of composition, something he was determined to do. He quickly had the machines repaired and put back in service for the Senate *Debates*. Then he ordered four additional linotypes from the Montreal Linotype Company, began training more operators and developed new applications for the machines.

These early linotypes were probably of the kind known as "star-base" machines, which had only one narrow magazine. Each machine was capable of producing a short line of type in only one size and style, of which Long Primer, or 11-point type, used for numerous official publications, was the largest. The lines of type were up to five inches long, which was ideal for setting the narrow columns of newspapers or

parliamentary debates. Dawson reasoned, however, that linotype machines would not meet the needs of the Printing Bureau unless they could be operated between sessions to set the wider columns required for the pages of annual reports and other departmental publications. But the machine's suitability for book work was not immediately evident. This was probably not because of the short line of type the machine produced, as Dawson thought, but more likely because the early machines could not easily produce the variety of type styles and sizes usually required for book work. Once a book had been set by linotype machine, a printer who then changed the matrix to work with a different type size, required much time and trouble to get the machine ready to recast corrected lines in the type size used for the job completed earlier.

The Printing Bureau, with masses of departmental book work to do in the same size and style of type, was in a unique position to demonstrate the linotype's adaptability to book work. This was accomplished in February 1892, when the Bureau issued the first pamphlet set by a linotype machine. Dawson considered that this accomplishment—the use of linotype machines for book printing—put his establishment ahead of any other printing office in Canada or elsewhere. The pamphlet was set in 10 or 11-point type (either Long Primer or Brevier), and was probably 24 picas, or four inches, wide. We know that it was printed for the Department of Agriculture, though, oddly enough, no one thought to record the title of this historic publication.

One further obstacle remained in the way of a complete transition to the linotype machine. Although the Senate *Debates* were still composed during the day, most other parliamentary publications, including the House of Commons *Hansard*, had to be set by compositors working the night shift, when the steam engines were shut down. As Dawson pointed out, it would have been uneconomical to run one of the large engines all night, just to generate the six horsepower required to operate the Bureau's battery of eight linotype machines. It is therefore unlikely that the House of Commons *Hansard* was set by machine before 1893, when George Low of Ottawa installed a 6 x 6 foot steam engine in the linotype room. By 1894, however, *Hansard* was set entirely by machine, and with good results. Local union Secretary C.S.O. Boudreault reported that operators were having no trouble keeping up with the debates, "no matter how long-winded the legislator may be."

Once the linotype machine's capabilities had been demonstrated, its importance at the Bureau increased rapidly. At first, machines were used mostly during sessions of Parliament and held in reserve for emergencies during part of the year. But additional work required by Parliament and the growing departments rapidly outpaced the capacity of the machines. By the turn of the century, the Bureau had ten late-model machines, which, during ten months of the year, were run night and day by separate shifts. In fact, Dawson insisted that the space limitations of the building were such that, without linotype machines, the Bureau would have been unable to keep up with the growing demand for printing.

In 1903, only 12 years after the first typesetting machinery was installed, the Bureau had 15 linotypes, and hand composition was gradually being limited to work such as tables and charts, which could not be set on the linotypes. It will put Dawson's achievements in perspective to note that United States Public Printer Frank W. Palmer was still unconvinced of the machine's "economy or adaptability." In 1904, Palmer purchased, for testing, a number of typesetting machines, with catastrophic repercussions. Public outrage over the cost of the machines and resistance from the craft, who believed their jobs were endangered, led to a bitter controversy. A study committee was set up, and in 1905 President Roosevelt released Palmer.

Of course, credit for the Canadian government printing office's successful introduction of typesetting machinery must go not only to the Queen's Printer, but also to the compositors who made such a pioneering transition possible. Some of them were among the first printers in Canada to learn these new skills.

According to a report in *The Inland Printer*, the rate for night work was $18 for a week of 50 hours; for day work, it was $15 for a 54-hour week. Nevertheless, the transition was not without hardship, at least at first. In 1893, the pay scale for linotype operators was adopted at the Bureau. During that year's parliamentary session, approximately 25 percent fewer compositors were employed than during the

previous session, when linotypes were not used for sessional work. Dawson's way of describing the situation was to say that linotypes had done away with the formerly heavy *suspensions* of temporary compositors *after* the session. But it can also be said that linotypes did away with the *hiring* of temporary compositors *during* the sessions.

However, compositors need not have feared long-term displacement, for it quickly became apparent at printing offices everywhere that skilled hand compositors became far more efficient machine operators than did those with no knowledge of the craft. In the words of Lee Reilly, a *New York Tribune* compositor who became well known for setting speed records on the new machines:

An operator requires to be a *printer* to be rapid and competent. The assumption has been that typewriters—or typewritists—as a rule, make competent operators of composing machines. This is a complete delusion. Such operators are failures in every sense of the word, and I speak from practical observation.

In the long run, the machines so stimulated the demand for printing that more work was done than ever before. "The voluminous Saturday and Sunday issues of the daily press," Dawson noted, "are striking indications of the changed conditions in the trade." And the requirements of the public service grew so quickly that the Printing Bureau was no exception.

. . . nowhere else in the world is there a service equal to the "Hansard" service at Ottawa. . . . Even on those occasions when the House sat continuously day and night for a week, the debates up to 3 o'clock in the morning were on the members' desks at 3 p.m. every day. The pamphlet of debates often reaches five forms or 80 pages of double column. . . . It is taken now as a matter of course, but there is nothing like it done elsewhere.

Samuel Edward Dawson, 1899

ueen's Printer Dawson was particularly proud of his establishment's *Hansard* service to Parliament, and never missed an opportunity to elaborate. He credited the House of Commons reporters and the Bureau's compositors and proofreaders with the accuracy of the service; but its speed, he attributed to the linotype machines.

The Queen's Printer was required to publish only parliamentary speeches made before midnight each day. But the rate of composition attained on the Printing Bureau's linotypes allowed a complete report of the previous day's debate to be on each member's desk before the following day's session began at 3 p.m. This was accomplished even when the House had not adjourned until 4 o'clock that morning. With characteristic confidence, Dawson announced, "If complaint be made, in Parliament or elsewhere, of delays in the issues of any of the Hansards, inquiry will always reveal the fact that such delay, if it exists, is not to be charged to the printers."

At the U.S. Government Printing Office, where linotypes were not yet in use, no speech appeared in the *Congressional Record* the following day if the printer received the copy after midnight. And Dawson was proud to point out that the British system would have been even less satisfactory in Canada. In Britain, the *Hansard* was still printed by a private contractor, who was allowed three days before sending even the first proofs to the members of Parliament. These were revised, and the speeches were finally published seven days after delivery.

Both the American and the British printed records suffered from what Dawson described as an additional weakness: unlike the Canadian *Hansard*, neither of them provided a verbatim account of the debates. In the United States, representatives and senators always enjoyed the right to revise or withhold

their remarks from the record and to supply the Public Printer with copy for speeches which were never delivered. In England, the rules for publication in *Hansard* were more precise, but reporters were permitted to summarize the speeches to one third of their original length.

Despite the Canadian *Hansard*'s relative excellence, in 1901 the Joint Committee on Printing decided to bring the service to "a higher degree of perfection" and inaugurated an important change. Based on encouraging consultation with the Queen's Printer, the Committee decided to publish each day's debate before 10 a.m., instead of at 3 o'clock in the afternoon.

"To get out the Hansard Debates at an early hour in the morning," Dawson ventured, "is, in reality, so far as the printing is concerned, nothing more than to adopt newspaper methods." In designing a new *Hansard* production routine along those lines, Dawson made the publication essentially what it is today.

Until this time, only compositors and proofreaders routinely worked a night shift at the Printing Bureau. The presses and the steam-powered bindery equipment all stopped at 5:30 p.m. each day when the steam engines were shut down. For the new *Hansard* schedule, Dawson geared the entire plant for round-the-clock production, which meant two work-shifts, since the operatives were required to work a nine or ten-hour day. Steam power was provided day and night, so that one or more presses could be kept running continuously. The proofreading staff was increased, and in the pressroom and pamphlet bindery night shifts were instituted. Under these conditions, an early morning edition of *Hansard* was successfully inaugurated.

According to Dawson, the news that "the world's finest Hansard service" had undergone further improvements caused considerable consternation at Westminster, among members of Britain's Parliament. One member wanted to know:

Why cannot the Imperial parliament give to its members what the Dominion government gives to its members? . . . I have found on careful inquiry and by an examination of the official reports that the Canadian parliament sits quite as late as our own— and indeed very much later. Notwithstanding this fact and the additional fact that the proceedings are conducted in two languages, members get the report of the proceedings on their breakfast table the next morning. If this can be done in Canada why cannot it be done in London? Are our printers less enterprising? Is it a matter of expense? Then surely if the Dominion parliament can afford it the Imperial parliament ought to be able to do so. It would be a great advantage to honourable members to be able to secure the answers to questions and to keep themselves *au courant* with the proceedings of the House. Are there not other directions in which economies might be made?

Two visits were paid to the establishment of the Queen's Printer, which is undoubtedly in a highly efficient and still improving condition. Great economies have been introduced in the management of the masses of printing and stationery required by the Government, and the erection of the building and the placing therein the improved machinery and quantity of type it contains has been amply justified by the result.

Report of the Royal Commissioners Appointed to Enquire into Certain Matters Relating to the Civil Service of Canada, 1892 ear by year in his reports to Parliament, Dawson marshalled bits of new evidence "to correct some misconceptions concerning the working of the Bureau which evidently exist in the minds of many." These misconceptions were concerned primarily with the cost and efficiency of work done at the Bureau. His most impressive effort was a 50-page document published in 1899, the Printing Bureau's tenth year in operation. It

167

The first page of Senate *Debates* printed from type set by machine. The Superintendent of Printing reported that linotype machines were used to set the Senate *Debates* even earlier, in 1891. But this was probably done on an experimental basis only, for examination of the printed volumes did not reveal any linotype composition prior to the opening of the Second Session of the Seventh Parliament, on February 25, 1892. Other pages from the printed record show that matter set by machine was interspersed with French-language copy, and with copy in smaller type sizes, both of which were still set by hand. By 1894, the *Debates* for both the Senate and the House of Commons were set entirely by machine.

contained Dawson's exhaustive analysis of all aspects of government printing and purported to resolve the matter of cost "beyond any shadow of doubt." Widely circulated and well-received, the report was favourably reviewed even in the printing trade journals, for Dawson knew how to convince as much by the sheer force of his polemics as by the intrinsic merit of the facts he presented.

During a five-month period in 1892, which included a parliamentary session, Dawson's office had taken note of every item of work delivered and, for comparison's sake, had prepared invoices on the basis of prices under the former contracts. These invoices were then compared with the actual prices charged to government departments by the Bureau. By this comparison, Dawson showed that if the departments and Parliament had paid contract rates, during a 12-month period, they would have spent some $40,000 more than the $289,000 they were actually paying for printing at the Bureau.

Though it could be charged that his figures, like Chamberlin's, still did not reflect the Bureau's true operating costs, Dawson had a cleverly contrived response. He reasoned that if the Bureau had been permitted to charge for standing matter, the rate charged by the contractors would have brought in additional revenue of more than $50,000 annually. This, he argued, would have covered the cost of power, light and other operating expenses easily, as well as interest payments on capital invested.

In support of his arguments, Dawson also provided specific examples of savings, based on the experiences of some of the larger departments. The Post Office was still paying an average of nine percent less per year for printing than it had under the contract system, even though business conducted in the various branches of this department had increased between 33 and 73 percent in ten years. He also cited *The Canadian Patent Office Record*, first printed at the Bureau in 1892. Previously, *The Record* had been prepared by a private printer, outside the departmental printing contract. Dawson claimed that annual savings on this publication alone "would more than pay the salaries of the Superintendent of Printing and all his clerks." He also noted that the Commissioner of Patents was as impressed by the journal's improved appearance as he was by the reduction in its cost.

Perhaps most interesting were Dawson's tables comparing the overall costs of printing under the contracts with costs at the Bureau. To arrive at the cost of printing under contract, he calculated not just what was paid to the contractors; he also included amounts recorded in the *Public Accounts* as having been paid outside the contract to other firms receiving government business. Calculated this way, the cost of printing at the Bureau between 1892 and 1897 averaged $2,704 per year less than it had averaged during the last five years of printing under the contracts despite the fact that, during the intervening ten years,

169

Turn-of-the-century views of the Printing Bureau.
The building's scenic location at Nepean Point in
Ottawa is now the site of Canada's National Gallery.

the amount of printing had increased by at least 75 percent!

In truth, Dawson's figures were almost as inconclusive as those of his predecessor, because complete statistics on the total cost of government printing, not just the cost of labour and materials, were still not available. Nevertheless, the evidence of ten years, bolstered by this Queen's Printer's impressive rhetoric, made it almost impossible to resist the conclusion that the Department of Public Printing and Stationery was producing not just improved work, but also substantial savings. Thus, Dawson concluded:

. . . a widely prevalent notion that it is impossible for a Government to make an economic success of such a manufacturing establishment as the Bureau. . . is based upon a want of faith in representative institutions rather than upon any inherent necessity of the case.

Indeed, Dawson was confident enough to renew an argument which Brown Chamberlin had first presented in 1884, but which the Secretary of State had subsequently played down during parliamentary debate. This was the notion that printing for the Canadian Parliament and for its various government departments was an essential service, important enough to the public welfare that the potential expense of a government-run manufacturing establishment should not be the primary concern. Citing government-run factories of military supplies, map-making establishments and paper mills in Britain, Dawson declared:

Matters of vital importance are not entrusted to the competition of private contract. When the lives of Her Majesty's soldiers and sailors, or the existence of Her Majesty's empire is involved, it is not thought desirable to rely upon the efficiency of private competition.

For the time being, and after years of effort, the Printing Bureau had at last earned a well-respected place among government services.

FURTHER READING

These notes are provided for readers who may be interested in obtaining more information, and to credit the historians, researchers and writers who have sought out and collected information that has been used in this narrative.

Both primary and secondary sources were used in compiling this book. Primary sources include various government records, private manuscripts and photographs held by the National Archives of Canada (NAC), and by other institutions and individuals. Further information came from interviews with departmental staff and descendants of former Queen's Printers and other officials, who often had photographs, as well as letters and other pertinent papers. The most important published sources of information were the parliamentary and other official publications available at the National Library of Canada (NLC).

Where secondary sources were available, particularly for the early chapters of the book, and for many of the biographical sketches, these have considerably lessened the laborious searches of government records and other primary source materials. Although many of these published works are out of print, they are still available for consultation in major reference libraries.

Since this is not an academic history, detailed references do not accompany the text. However, sources of information are often identified directly within the story. Other sources, whether primary or secondary, are listed under the titles of chapters to which they are most relevant. In addition, the following sources were consulted repeatedly:

For information on the technology and craft of printing, see the comprehensive guide, *The Printing Industry*, by Victor Strauss (Printing Industries of America, Inc., 1967). Another interesting source, more historical in its approach, is the *Canadian Book of Printing* published by Toronto Public Libraries (Toronto, 1940). For a history of government service from before Confederation, see *The Civil Service of Canada* by Robert MacGregor Dawson (Oxford University Press, 1929).

Information about the various types of publications issued by Parliament and the departments and agencies of the federal government, and about the kind of material which they contain, is to be found in *Canadian Official Publications* by Olga Bernice Bishop (Pergamon Press, 1981). Marion Villiers Higgins' bibliography, *Canadian Government Publications. A Manual for Librarians* (American Library Association, 1935) provides outline histories of various federal government departments, bodies and agencies, and lists of publications from 1841 to the early 1930s. For current information about federal government publications, see the catalogues published by the Queen's Printer for Canada. They may be consulted at libraries and associated bookstores, or ordered directly from the Canadian Government Publishing Centre of the Department of Supply and Services. The *Weekly Checklist of Canadian Government Publications* is the most up-to-date listing of all free and priced publications released during the previous week. These *Checklists* are indexed and compiled into a permanent reference source, *The Quarterly Catalogue of Government of Canada Publications*. The yearly, annotated catalogue, *Selected Titles*, lists a wide variety of the most popular priced publications, while a series of nine *Subject Lists* provides comprehensive bibliographies of priced government publications related to particular subjects.

Introduction: Printing for the Nation

Information about printing and publishing in **Printers and Politicians** was provided by Canadian Government Printing Services and by the Canadian Government Publishing Centre. Historical statistics are from *Department of Public Printing and Stationery Annual Report* (hereafter *DPPS*), *for the Year Ending 30th June, 1891*. **Printing the *Hansard*** was compiled from interviews with staff, and from internal departmental records. For a history of this publication, see *The Hansard Chronicles* by John Ward (Deneau and Greenberg, 1980).

Part I. By Commission

Lieutenant-Governor Simcoe's Statement about the importance of a printer, which introduces **Early Government Printers**, is from *The Correspondence of Lieut. Governor John Graves Simcoe, Volume I,* collected and edited by Brigadier General E.A. Cruikshank, LL.D., F.R.S.C. (Ontario Historical Society, 1923). Information about the first Canadian printing press in Nova Scotia, and about early printing in the colony of Quebec and in Upper Canada, was taken from various published accounts. For the full story of the arrival of the printing press in all provinces, see *The Introduction of Printing into Canada* by Aegidius Fauteux (Montreal, 1930); *Early Printing in Canada* by Marie Tremaine (Toronto, 1937); or *The Spread of Printing. Western Hemisphere. Canada* by H. Pearson Gundy (Routledge & Kegan Paul, 1972). Eric Hawthorne's particularly readable account, *Imprint of a Nation*, contains the story of Bushell's inauspicious debut used in **Canada's First Government Printer**. Isaiah Thomas' remarks about Bushell and Henry are in his study, *The History of Printing in America with a Biography of Printers in two volumes* (New York, 1874). H. Pearson Gundy quotes the rebuke Mesplet received from Lieutenant-Governor Simcoe's office in *Early Printers and Printing in the Canadas*

(Bibliographical Society of Canada, 1957). The history and operation of the Upper Canada printing press are described in "Press of the Olden Time," "An Old Hand Press," and "Printed the U.C. Gazette," in J. Ross Robertson's *Landmarks of Toronto*, Fifth Series (Toronto, 1908). *A Bibliography of Canadian Imprints 1751-1800* by Marie Tremaine (University of Toronto Press, 1952), is a standard reference work to early publications.

The text of Desbarats and Derbishire's joint appointment as Queen's Printer to the United Province of Canada is in the Register of Commissions and Letters Patent of the Province of Canada (NAC, RG68 Liber17 folio14, 30 September 1841, on microfilm reel C-3927). Olga Bernice Bishop's *Publications of the Government of the Province of Canada 1841-1867* (National Library of Canada, 1963), contains a comprehensive bibliography and a general discussion of government printing during the period. The petitions from official printers to the provinces of Upper and Lower Canada, and the response from Govenor Metcalfe, are recorded in the State Minute Books (NAC, RG1 E1, Canada State Book B, 29 June 1843, on microfilm reel C-110).

The biographical sketch, **George-Paschal Desbarats: A Family Dynasty**, is based on Peter Desbarats' introduction to *Canadian Illustrated News. A Commemorative Portfolio* (McClelland and Stewart, 1970), and on Aileen Desbarats' article in the *Dictionary of Canadian Biography (DCB)* VOL.IX. (University of Toronto Press, 1976). Obituaries in *The Globe* (Toronto), the *Daily Citizen* (Ottawa) and the *Montreal Gazette* were also consulted.

Much biographical detail about **Stewart Derbishire** was provided by family descendents Stewart Hughes and his mother, Frances Hughes, of Ottawa. Several contemporary biographies were consulted, most importantly the one in George MacLean Rose's *A Cyclopaedia of Canadian Biography: Being Chiefly Men of the Time* Vol. 2 (Toronto, 1888). Rose quotes Derbishire as wishing to see the fun of further rebellion. The letter in which Derbishire asked Durham for an assignment is in the Lord Durham Papers (NAC, MG24 A27 vol.37, on microfilm reel C-1858). "Stewart Derbishire's report to Lord Durham on Lower Canada, 1938," is edited by Norah Story and published in *Canadian Historical Review,* XVIII (1937). Derbishire's claim that Lord Sydenham arranged his appointment as Queen's Printer is in a letter he wrote to Dr. Alexander James Christie, editor of the *Bytown Gazette*, in the Hill Collection (NAC, MG24 I9 vol.5). For another perspective, see the article by Michael S. Cross, in *DCB* VOL.IX.

Derbishire's comment about the profitable nature of his commission, which heads the chapter entitled, **The Queen's Printer: Most Expensive Luxury About the Capital?** is in the Hill Collection (NAC, MG24 I9 vol.5, 5 October 1841). The description of the Queen's printership as the capital's most expensive luxury is taken from a debate in the House of Commons, 26 March 1868, recorded in the "Scrapbook Debates" in the Library of Parliament. The general survey of the arrangements Parliament made for printing is based on O.B. Bishop's *Publications of the Government of the Province of Canada 1841-1867*. The report of the Committee on Printing of the Legislative Assembly is in *Appendix to the Tenth Volume of the Journals of the Legislative Assembly*, 15 Vic., 1851. App. (D.D.), "Fifth Report of the Standing Committee on Printing"; that of the Joint Committee on Printing of both Houses, in *Appendix to the Seventeenth Volume of the Journals of the Legislative Assembly*, 22 Vic., 1859. App. (No. 57.), "Fifth Report of the Joint Committee on Printing". The recommendation to reform the Queen's Printer's commission following the death of G.P. Desbarats is in the State Minutes (NAC, RG1 E1, Canada State Book AA, 15 November 1864, on microfilm reel

C-121). The text of Desbarats and Cameron's joint appointment is in the Register of Commissions and Letters Patent of the Province of Canada (NAC, RG68 Liber30 folio 171, 20 April 1863, on microfilm reel C-3929).

The biographical sketch of **Malcolm Cameron** was compiled primarily from Margaret Coleman's article in *DCB* VOL.X, and from several contemporary biographies, most importantly, the entry in John Charles Dent, *The Canadian Portrait Gallery* Vol.4 (John B. Magurn, 1881), and George MacLean Rose, *A Cyclopaedia of Canadian Biography* Vol.1 (Toronto, 1886). Cameron's descriptions of himself as gritty and as a radical, and the quotation about his uncompromising nature, were taken from an obituary in the *Daily Citizen* (Ottawa). The Ogden Autograph Collection (NAC, MG24 C19) contains a photograph of Abraham Lincoln, with an admiring inscription in Cameron's hand.

The comment about G.P. Desbarats' exceptional management of **The Peripatetic Printshop** is from an obituary in *The Gazette*. Most of the information about Desbarats and Derbishire's Kingston and Montreal establishments, including the business statement, was taken from the reports of the committees on printing cited above. The suggestion from Derbishire and Desbarats for reducing the cost of printing, which heads this chapter, is taken from the "Fifth Report of the Joint Committee on Printing" of 1859. Information about Cunnabell's Halifax press is from D.C. Harvey's "Newspapers of Nova Scotia," *Canadian Historical Review* XXIV (1945), and is cited by George Parker in *The Beginnings of the Book Trade in Canada* (University of Toronto Press, 1985). Parker also mentions Lovell's acquisition of a steam press in 1847, which he believes was the first in Canada East. Romaine's claim that he was first to use steam printing in Canada is in the *Journals of the House of Commons*, 47 Vic., 1884. App. (No. 4), "Fifth and Seventh Reports of the Joint Committee on Printing."

Sir Edmund Head's recommendation of Ottawa as capital, cited in **From Independent Printer to Civil Servant**, is taken from *The Queen's Choice* by Wilfried Eggleston (Queen's Printer and Controller of Stationery, 1961). Manuscript Report 106, *Lower Town Ottawa* Vol. 2 *1854-1900*, by Michael Newton (National Capital Commission, 1981), contains a description of the Desbarats Block. Details about the printshop and the fire are taken from the *Daily Citizen* (Ottawa), 29 January 1869, and *The Ottawa Times*, 21 and 22 January 1869. The Fenian crisis in Ottawa, the assassination of McGee, and the burning of Desbarats Block are all described in *Recollections* by Lilian Scott Desbarats (Ottawa, 1957), and in *Canadian Illustrated News. A Commemorative Portfolio* by Peter Desbarats, which also contains the excerpts from Lucianne Desbarats' diary. **The Civil Service Up in Arms** contains information from the *Report on the State of the Militia of the Province of Canada for the Year 1867* (Ottawa, 1868). The quotations are taken from a pamphlet, *Standing Orders of the Civil Service Rifle Regiment* (Ottawa, 1866). J.A. Macdonald's letter offering G.E. Desbarats the Queen's Printer's appointment, which was also used to introduce this chapter, is in the J. A. Macdonald Letters (NAC, MG26A Vol.573 File 4, 24 May 1869).

Information about **George Edward Desbarats: The Dominion's First Queen's Printer**, and about the significance of his work with **William Augustus Leggo: Desbarats' Partner,** is taken from Peter Desbarats' introduction to *Canadian Illustrated News. A Commemorative Portfolio.*

A report of Chamberlin's marriage to Agnes Dunbar Moodie appeared in *The Ottawa Times*, 15 June 1870. The letter from B. Chamberlin asking the Prime Minister for an appointment is in the J.A. Macdonald Letters (NAC, MG26A, Vol.342, pp. 156582-3). **Brown Chamberlin: Longest Serving Queen's Printer** is based on several contemporary biographies, most importantly, the entries in George MacLean Rose,

A Cyclopaedia of Canadian Biography Vol.1, in Henry James Morgan, *The Canadian Men and Women of the Time: A Hand-book of Canadian Biography* (William Briggs, 1898), and *Canadian Illustrated News*, 25 June 1870. Obituaries in the *Daily Citizen (Ottawa), The Gazette* (Montreal) and *The Journal* (Ottawa) were also consulted. Agnes Dunbar Moodie is entered as "Mrs. Brown Chamberlin" in Henry J. Morgan's *Types of Canadian Women Past and Present* (William Briggs, 1903). **How the Queen's Printer Became a Hero** was compiled from reports in the *Canadian Illustrated News*, 4 and 11 June 1870; and from the *Report on the State of the Militia of the Dominion of Canada for the Year 1870* (Ottawa, 1871), which contains Chamberlin's account of his actions.

Part II: Under Contract

The rhyme at the head of **Partial Reform: The Contract System** appears in A.J. Magurn's article, "Canada's Government Printing Bureau," in *The Inland Printer*, Vol.10, No.3, February 1892. The contracts, and G.E. Desbarats' comments on the subject, were printed in the *Sessional Papers* (No. 46) Session 1870.

The descriptions of **The Queen's Printer's Branch**, and **The Government Stationery Office**, are based on annual reports Chamberlin and Young submitted to Parliament through the Secretary of State; and on "The Civil Service," in *The Ottawa Free Press*, 19 January 1878. Chamberlin's analysis of Post Office printing costs is attached to an order of the Privy Council.

G.E. Desbarats' opinion of the low prices heading **Woes of a Contractor: Taylor's Trials** was taken from the sessional paper cited above. The account of Taylor's problems was compiled primarily from information found in the "Scrapbook Debates" available in the Library of Parliament, and from reports of the Joint Committee on the Printing of Parliament, between 1869 and 1874, most importantly *Journals of the House of Commons*, 36 Vic., 1873, App. (No. 1), "Fifth Report of the Joint Committee of Both Houses on the Printing of Parliament." Advances paid Taylor, and increases to his contract rates, are in the Records of the Privy Council Office. The Queen's Printer's 1872 report records James Cotton's failure to live up to the terms of the paper-supply contract. The report for 1873 mentions that a strike of Ottawa printers lasted from 24 July to 3 October of that year. **Printers' Inklings: A Family Tradition** is based on family papers in the possession of William Armstrong's grandson, Gordon Victor Armstrong.

As mentioned in the text, **More Lice in the Type: Patronage and Confidential Printing** is based almost entirely on debate in the House of Commons, and on reports of the Joint Committee on the Printing of Parliament. The comments from the printing trade were taken from *The Printer's Miscellany* (Saint John): Vol.I, No.4, October 1876; and "Centralization," Vol.II, No.12, June 1878. **Putting on the Pious: Bogus Offers and the End of Contracts** is taken from the *Journals of the House of Commons*, 43 Vic., 1880, App. (No. 2), "Thirteenth Report of the Joint Committee on Printing." **Planning for Canada's Printing Requirements** is taken from Chamberlin's report on government printing, which forms part of his report to the Secretary of State for 1884. Robert Romaine's observations, and the recommendations of the Joint Committee on Printing, are in the "Fifth and Seventh Reports of the Joint Committee on Printing" for 1884, cited earlier, under the **The Peripatetic Printshop.**

The Department of Public Printing and Stationery is based on Parliament's debate of Bill 132, introduced 12 May 1886. The quotations were all taken from the *Debates of the House of Commons*. **A Great Day for Brown Chamberlin** is based on a report in *The Evening Journal* (Ottawa), 17 July 1886, which quotes Chamberlin's remarks on his new position. The names of the employees were taken from a pay list in a departmental record book.

Part III: By Government

Years of Turmoil: Building the Printing Plant, cites a letter, from the Secretary of State to the Prime Minister, about the proposed site for the building, from the J.A. Macdonald Letters (NAC, MG26A Vol.205, 8 July 1886). The construction specifications are in the Records of the Department of Public Works (NAC, RG11 Contract No. 1127, 6 June 1886). Construction costs and delays are described in *DPPS* (1887-1889). Biographical information about André Senécal was taken from *The Canadian Parliamentary Companion* (J. Drurie & Son, 1891), and from testimony given before the Select Standing Committee on Public Accounts, and printed in the *Report and Minutes of Evidence in Connection with the Government Printing Bureau* (Brown Chamberlin, Printer to the Queen's Most Excellent Majesty, 1891).

Printers' Pride: First Permanent Home. The date Senécal completed the move to the new building is recorded in *DPPS*, 1889. John Lovell's remarks are taken from the Select Standing Committee on Public Accounts, *Report and Minutes of Evidence in Connection with the Government Printing Bureau*. Dawson's assessment of the building, which heads this chapter, is in *DPPS*, 1891. The story about the near-collapse of MacLean, Roger's building surfaced in testimony before the *Royal*

Commission of Inquiry on the Relations between Capital and Labour in Canada. Evidence-Ontario (Ottawa, 1889). The Printing Bureau building is described in the *Report of the Minister of Public Works for the Fiscal Year Ended 30th June 1887*, and on the contract specifications in the Records of the Department of Public Works.

The descriptions of various sections of the plant, of its equipment and type, in **Working in the New Printing Bureau**, were compiled from *DPPS*, 1889, and from a variety of other sources: A.J. Magurn's article, "Canada's Government Printing Bureau" in *The Inland Printer*; reports of the *Auditor General*; the *Public Accounts*; and testimony given before the Select Standing Committee on Public Accounts during the 1891 inquiry into the Printing Bureau. John Lovell's remark heading this chapter was also taken from evidence presented before this committee. Technical descriptions of the printing presses in **At the Heart of the Operation**, of **Stereotyping**, and of devices and processes in **The Bindery**, are taken from Harold E. Sterne's *Catalogue of Nineteenth Century Printing Presses* (1978), and *Catalogue of Nineteenth Century Bindery Equipment* (1978). Both publications are available from the publisher, Ye Olde Printery, 5815 Cherokee Drive, Cincinnati, Ohio 45243. **Supplying Stationery and Distributing Government Publications** is based on *DPPS*, and on the Records of the Privy Council Office.

Printers' Pride or Boodle Bureau? is based on the report of the Select Standing Committee on Public Accounts cited under **Three More Years of Turmoil**, and on newspaper accounts of the inquiry. Biographical information about **Samuel Edward Dawson** was taken from contemporary biographies and obituaries. The observation about Dawson's patriotism was made by A.P. Coleman, in a book review. Dawson's rebuke about the pocket knives is in a letter he wrote to Joseph Pope (NAC, MG30 E86 Vol.7 File Q, 24 December 1894); his assertion that he wrote a book about Canada for British readers, in a letter to J.E. Roy, President of the Royal Society (NAC, MG29 D83, 29 October 1908). Dawson's involvement with Renouf, and his activities relating to copyright, are discussed in George L. Parker, *The Beginnings of the Book Trade in Canada*.

Senécal and Chamberlin's purchase of linotype machines in New York, recorded in **A New Era: Composition by Machine**, was taken from *DPPS*, 1891. That the Senate *Debates* were temporarily printed by machine in 1891 came out in testimony before the Select Standing Committee on Public Accounts. The date that union records mention typesetting machinery at *The Globe* is mentioned by Sally Zerker in *The Rise and Fall of the Toronto Typographical Union* (Toronto, 1982). Dawson's account of the printing of a pamphlet, and of the *Hansard*, by linotype, is in the departmental annual reports. The dates of installations of linotype machinery, and of the steam engine to run it, are recorded in the annual reports of the *Auditor General*. Events surrounding the introduction of typesetting machines in the U.S. Government Printing Office are described in *100 GPO Years 1861-1961* by James L. Harrison (Washington, D.C., n.d.). Lee Reilly's remarks about competent typesetters appears in *The Inland Printer*, Vol.12, No.6, March 1894. **A Hansard Service "Unequalled in Any Part of the World"** and **Into the Twentieth Century** were compiled entirely from information contained in *DPPS*. Dawson's statement heading the former section comes from *DPPS*, 1898.

PHOTO CREDITS

12 *Clockwise from top:*
House of Commons
0904-313 N244/CGPS/
CGPS/CGPS

24 National Archives of
Canada (NAC), CI33550

25 NAC, C26248

26 National Museum of
Science and Technology
(NMST)

28 McCord Museum of Cana-
dian History

30 Mary Anne Jackson-Hughes,
Kanata

34 National Library of
Canada (NL), NL16259

36 NAC, C37045

38 NL

39 Notman Photographic
Archives, McCord Museum
of Canadian History
(NPA), 20148-II

40 NAC, C64270

44 NAC, C2726

50 *Left to right:*
NMST/NAC, PA51846

52 Edward J. Anderson
Collection, Toronto

54 *Left to right:*
NAC, PA51832/Bytown
Museum, Ottawa

55 NPA, 60890-I

56 Bytown Museum

58 NAC, C48503

59 *Left to right:*
NL15108/NAC, C79300

60 William James Topley,
NAC, PA145314

61 NAC, C48837

62 NAC, PA145315

63 NL16272

68 NAC, C117839

70 NL15112

71 NAC, PA26652

76 NL15114

79 NL

84 NAC, C62594

86 NL

87 NL16243

89 NL15107

92 NL16229

108 Bytown Museum

110 NAC, PA27057

111 NAC, PA145313

114 NAC, C3812

116 *Left to right:*
NAC, RG11, Volume
3916, C130521/C130520

120 NAC, PA144960

129 Harold Sterne, Cincinnati

131 Sterne

134 *From top:*
NL15343/Sterne

135 Sterne

136 Sterne

138 Sterne

139 Sterne

142 *Left to right:*
Peter Larochelle,
Ottawa/CGPS

146 NL

149 Ottawa Public Library

154 NPA, 55591-BII

158 *Left to right:*
The Inland Printer,
January 1909,
NMST/NAC, PA144958

160 *American Printer*, 1912,
NMST

168 *Left to right:*
NL16269/NL16268/
NL16270

170 *Clockwise from top:*
CGPS/NAC, P8373/
CGPS/CGPS

All other illustrations courtesy
Canadian Government
Printing Services (CGPS).